THE F

AHMADIYYA MOVEMENT

A SHORT STUDY

BY

HAZRAT MAULANA MUHAMMAD ALI, M.A.. LL.B

World-famous author of:
An English Translation of the Holy Qur'an
with Commentary and Text
The Religion of Islam
A Manual of Hadith
and many other works

AHMADIYYA ANJUMAN ISHA'AT ISLAM, LAHORE, INC.
36911 Walnut Street, Newark
CA 94560, USA

First published in present form 1937
Third Edition 1984

Published by Ahmadiyya Anjuman Isha'at Islam,
Lahore, Inc.
36911 Walnut Street
Newark, CA   94560

ISBN #0-913321-64-8

Typeset by Linguatype Limited,
Slough, Berks, England

C O N T E N T S

Hazrat Mirza GHULAM AHMAD of Qadian
The Promised Messiah and Mahdi
Founder of the Ahmadiyya Movement

FOREWORD

MAULANA MUHAMMAD ALI AND THE FOUNDER OF THE AHMADIYYA MOVEMENT

MAULANA MUHAMMAD ALI (1874-1951) is well-known all over the world as the author of several magnificent books on Islam, including the voluminous pioneer work, the *English Translation of the Holy Qur'an with Commentary*. His writings, covering all aspects of the Islamic faith, whether doctrinal, historical, contemporary or moral, have been showered with accolades by Muslims and non-Muslims alike for guiding millions of people around the globe towards Islam during this century.

As the late *Maulana* acknowledged in the prefaces to many of his books, the man who drew him into the field of religion, the source of his inspiration, his mentor and guide, and the fountain-head of the new thought expounded by him, was the Founder of the Ahmadiyya Movement, *Hazrat*[1] Mirza Ghulam Ahmad of Qadian (may God's mercy be upon him!). Sadly, the life and teachings of this great Muslim Reformer and thinker have been misunderstood and misrepresented beyond all limits. It is extremely fortunate, therefore, that Maulana Muhammad Ali recorded this concise biography of his master, an account which is highly authoritative, not only

1. *Hazrat*: an Arabic word, used by speakers of Urdu and Persian as an honorific title for a Muslim holy man.

account which is highly authoritative, not only
because of the Maulana's established reputation as
a scholar of the highest merit and integrity, but
also because he was a close associate and confidant
of Hazrat Mirza *Sahib* [2], living and working with him
in Qadian for the last nine years of the Founder's
life.

It was at the behest of Hazrat Mirza Sahib that
Maulana Muhammad Ali, having obtained qualifi-
cations in English and Law, dedicated his life for
the cause of Islam about the year 1900 and came to
join the Founder in Qadian. At the very outset,
Hazrat Mirza Sahib expressed the following opinion
about him:

"I am very pleased that another righteous young
man has joined our community by the grace of
God, namely, Maulvi Muhammad Ali, M.A.,
Advocate. I have very high hopes of him. I am
sure that my prediction will not go wrong that
this young man will make progress in the path of
God, and set such examples of being firm in
righteousness and love of the faith as ought to be
followed by his fellows" (4 October 1899; see
Majmu'a Ishtiharat; vol. viii, p. 68).

Settling in Qadian, Maulana Muhammad Ali
continued to translate various booklets and tracts
for Hazrat Mirza Sahib, as he had been doing since
joining the Movement in 1897. Then, in 1901, the
Founder decided to start an English journal, *The*

2. *Sahib*: an Arabic word meaning, literally, "friend" or "companion",
used in Indian languages as a title or form of address like "Mr", or "Sir".

Review of Religions, to present the true picture of
Islam to the Western world. He appointed Maulana
Muhammad Ali as the editor. In this magazine,
besides his own contributions, the Maulana also
translated articles and discourses by Hazrat Mirza
Sahib. The periodical soon acquired fame and
renown for the high quality of its contents,
scholarship and eloquence. In this connection, the
following item appeared in the diary columns of the
Ahmadiyya community's newspaper, *Badr*, in its
issue for 15 November 1906:

"*The Review of Religions* was being mentioned.
Someone praised it, saying that its articles were
of a high order. Hazrat Mirza said: 'Its editor is
Maulvi Muhammad Ali, a capable and scholarly
man with a religious bent of mind. His name had
gone forward for the E.A.C. [a prestigious Civil
Service post], but he left all that to settle here.
That is why God has blessed his writings.'"

Another recorded incident, published at the time,
shows the perfect confidence Hazrat Mirza Sahib
had in Maulana Muhammad Ali as being a true and
reliable exponent of his teachings and claims:

"Hazrat Mirza called in the editors of *Al-Hakam*
and *Al-Badr* [Ahmadiyya community's news-
papers] and instructed them to be very careful
in transcribing his speeches and articles, lest
something be misreported . . . So it was proper
(added Hazrat Mirza) that they show such
articles to Maulvi Muhammad Ali before

publication" (Diary Notes for 2 November 1902, *Malfuzat Ahmadiyya*, vol. vii, p. 445).

In his Divine mission of the propagation of Islam to the West too, Hazrat Mirza Sahib regarded Maulana Muhammad Ali as his most capable representative. He once said:

"I wish to write a book on the teachings of Islam, and Maulvi Muhammad Ali should translate it" (*Manzur Ilahi*, p. 188).

On another occasion, he directed the Maulana to write a comprehensive work presenting to the West the true picture of Islam as revealed to him in this age:

"On 13 February 1907, *Hazrat Aqdas* [Hazrat Mirza Sahib] called in Maulvi Muhammad Ali and told him that he wanted to fulfil his obligation of the propagation of Islam to the Western people by having an English book written. 'This is your task . . . it is these people's right to have the true Islam shown to them which God has made manifest to me, and they should be informed of the distinctive features which God has placed in this Movement'" (*Badr*, 21 February 1907).

(It was some thirty years later, long after Hazrat Mirza Sahib had passed away, that Maulana Muhammad Ali completed this task magnificently by writing the monumental work *The Religion of Islam*. See also the Preface to that book.)

In December 1905, Hazrat Mirza Sahib published a pamphlet known as "The Will", in which he set out the arrangements for the management of the Movement after him. He constituted a central executive body, the *Sadr Anjuman Ahmadiyya*, to have charge of the Movement, and appointed Maulana Muhammad Ali to the key position of Secretary. This system came into operation at once, and thus, during the last two and a half years of the Founder's life, the Maulana held the chief administrative post in the Ahmadiyya Movement.

In May 1908, Hazrat Mirza Ghulam Ahmad passed away, and thus ended the period of nine years in which Maulana Muhammad Ali had lived and worked closely with the great Reformer as his beloved, devoted follower and one of the most prominent men in the Movement. The spiritual association between the master and the disciple was, however, not ended, as Hazrat Mirza Sahib saw in one of his visions relating to the after-life:

"I saw Maulvi Muhammad Ali in a vision. [I said to him:] 'You too were righteous and of pure intentions. So come and sit by my side'" (*Badr*, vol. iii, no. 29).

Some years earlier, Hazrat Mirza Sahib had written a touching letter to the Maulana as follows:

"I hold extremely good opinions about you. This is why I have a special love for you. If your nature had not been so pure in the sight of God, I could never have thought so well of you, never. I love you fervently from the bottom of my heart, and often pray for you in the five daily prayers" (facsimile of original Urdu letter, reproduced in *Mujahid-i Kabir*, p. 50).

And he had once given the Maulana the following testimonial, published in the Ahmadiyya community's newspaper *Al-Hakam* at the time:

"I wish that people like Maulvi Muhammad Ali could be produced. There is no certainty of life, and he is all alone with no one to help him or take his place" (Diary Column in *Al-Hakam*, 30 November 1905).

It was after the death of Hazrat Mirza Sahib that Maulana Muhammad Ali expanded his literary activities and over a period of four decades wrote the numerous English and Urdu books which gave him international renown. He also became head of the Ahmadiyya Anjuman Isha'at Islam, Lahore, and channeled the energies of a whole community towards the propagation of Islam throughout the world. This legendary story can be read more fully in the Maulana's abridged English biography[3] or in much greater detail in the Urdu version[4]. The purpose of this note has been to give the reader a glimpse of his close association with Hazrat Mirza Ghulam Ahmad and his prominent position in the

---

3. *Muhammad Ali - The Great Missionary of Islam*, by Mumtaz Ahmad Faruqui (Ahmadiyya Anjuman Isha'at Islam, Lahore, 1966).

4. *Mujahid-i Kabir* ("The Great Fighter for Islam"), Urdu biography of Maulana Muhammad Ali by his son Muhammad Ahmad and Mumtaz Ahmad Faruqui.

Movement during the Founder's lifetime. It is thus seen that Maulana Muhammad Ali, with his knowledge and experience, was in a unique position of authority to give an accurate and authentic account of the life, mission and teachings of the Founder of the Ahmadiyya Movement.

November 1983   *The Publishers*

THE FIRST FORTY YEARS

Family History

HAZRAT MIRZA GHULAM AHMAD, the founder of
the Ahmadiyya movement, was born at Qadian, a
village in the Gurdaspur District, Punjab, in 1836.[1]
His father's name was Mirza Ghulam Murtaza, and
the family is descended from the Barlas tribe [2] of
the Moghul family. His ancestors had long resided in
Khurasan, a province of Persia, and were the digni-
taries of the land. In the tenth century of the
Hijra, when Babar ruled India, one of his ancestors,
Mirza Hadi Beg, emigrated from Persia, most
probably on account of some family dissensions, and
with his family and about two hundred attendants

1. In the first edition of this book, 1839 was given as the date, and this
is also the date given by the founder himself in the short autobiography
which he wrote in 1897 and which appeared in his book *Al-Kitab al-
Bariyya*. This was, however, a guess, as there is no written record of the
exact date of his birth. Further on in this same autobiography, he states
that he passed nearly forty years of his life with his father, whose death
took place in 1876. On this basis, 1837 or 1836 would appear to be a
more probable date. His son, Mirza Bashir Ahmad, has produced strong
arguments in favour of 1836 as the year of his father's birth.

Publisher's Note: Further research has shown that the date of the
Founder's birth was most probably 13 February 1835.

2. This tribe was descended from Haji Barlas. He lived at Kush, to the
south of Samarqand, but was expelled from there by Taimur when he
conquered that land. Haji Barlas took shelter in Khurasan, and the
family lived there till they came over to India, in the time of Babar. On
account of their long residence in Persia, the Barlas tribe may be
included among the Persians. Some authorities, however, say that Barlas
is not a Moghul but a Persian tribe, as both *Barlas* and *Mirza* (the sur-
title) are words of Persian and not of Turkish origin. Hazrat Mirza
Ghulam Ahmad himself says that his ancestors were Persians.

sought refuge in India. Settling in a vast and fertile sub-Himalayan plain, called the Majjha, he there built a village, about 70 miles from Lahore in a north-easterly direction, and called it Islampur. The ruling monarch granted him a vast tract of land as a *jagir* with the right to exercise the powers of a *Qadzi* (*lit.*, a *magistrate*) or chief executive authority. Hence, Islampur became known as Islampur Qadi Majjhi, ultimately shortened to Qadi,[3] and at last became known as Qadian.

In the latter days of the Moghul Empire, when it was undergoing the process of dissolution, the *jagir* granted to the ancestors of Hazrat Ahmad[4] became an independent state. In the early days of the Sikh rule, when anarchy and oppression were the order of the day and Islam and the Muslims were being persecuted everywhere, Qadian remained for a long time the centre of peace and prosperity. Mirza Gul Muhammad, the great-grandfather of Hazrat Ahmad, was then the head of the family and, after the manner of the good Oriental chiefs, his purse was open for the learned and his table ministered freely to the poor and to the strangers. He had only eighty-five villages in his possession but, on account of his great love for piety and learning, many of the learned men who could not find shelter

3. The name *Kad'a*, which is only another form of *Qadi* or *Kadi*, is mentioned in a hadith of the Holy Prophet Muhammad as the place of the appearance of Mahdi (*Jawahir al-Asrar*, p. 55).

4. The shortened name Ahmad is adopted instead of the full name *Hazrat Mirza Ghulam Ahmad* for the sake of brevity. This is the name which he adopted in taking *bai'a* (oath of fealty), though in all his letters and writings he used his full name. In his revelations, both the long and the shortened forms occur; the following reason for this is from his own pen: "As being the manifestation of the Holy Prophet, I was called Ahmad, though my name was Ghulam Ahmad" (*Review of Religions*, vol. ii, p. 437).

elsewhere felt assured of a warm reception at Qadian. After the death of Mirza Gul Muhammad, his son, Mirza 'Ata Muhammad, became the chief, but he was soon overpowered by the Sikhs, who seized village after village until not a single village, except Qadian, was left in his possession. This place was strongly fortified, but a body of Sikhs, called Ram Garhis, made an entry into the town under false pretences and took possession of the village. Mirza 'Ata Muhammad and his whole family were made prisoners and deprived of their possessions. Their houses and the mosques were made desolate, and the library was burned to the ground. After inflicting all kinds of torture, the Sikhs ordered the family to leave the village of Qadian. Thus, expelled from their home, they sought shelter in another state, where 'Ata Muhammad was poisoned by his enemies. In the latter days of Ranjit Singh's ascendancy, Mirza Ghulam Murtaza obtained five villages from the *jagir* of his ancestors and re-settled at Qadian. Below is reproduced the opening paragraph of Sir Lepel Griffin's account of the family, published in the *Punjab Chiefs*:

"In 1530, the last year of the Emperor Babar's reign, Hadi Beg, a Mughal of Samarqand, emigrated to the Punjab and settled in Gurdaspur District. He was a man of some learning, and was appointed Kazi or Magistrate over seventy villages in the neighbourhood of Kadian, which town he is said to have founded, naming it Islampur Kazi, from which Kadian has by a natural change arisen. For several generations the family has held offices of respectability under the Imperial Government, and it was only when the Sikhs became powerful that it fell into poverty."

The Sikh anarchy was, soon after Hazrat Ahmad's birth, replaced by the peace and security of the British rule, and the Punjab Muslims once more breathed freely. The family naturally welcomed the change, and Mirza Ghulam Murtaza showed his staunch loyalty to the British rule in the Mutiny of 1857. In recognition of his services, he received a handsome pension and was highly esteemed by the officials.

Hazrat Ahmad's own impressions of the Sikh misrule and the persecution of Muslims were deep-seated, and he always spoke of the coming of the British as a blessing and as saving the Punjab Muslims from slavery and annihilation. It is for this matter-of-fact statement, which finds frequent expression in his writings, that he has been criticised by a certain school of politicians, who, therefore, regard him as favouring an alien government.

Education

In his childhood, Hazrat Mirza Ghulam Ahmad received his education at home. He learned the Holy Qur'an and some Persian books from a tutor named Fazl Ilahi, and later on some books on Arabic grammar from another tutor, named Fazl Ahmad. When he was seventeen or eighteen years old, a third tutor, Gul Ali Shah, was employed to teach him the ordinary Arabic textbooks of those days. He also studied some works on medicine from his father, who was a famous physician in his time.

Righteous and God-fearing

From his early days, Hazrat Ahmad had studious habits and he loved to remain in seclusion with his books. His father was, on that account, very anxious about him and repeatedly asked him to leave his seclusion and books for the more practical business of life, by which he meant that he should assist him in carrying out the plans which he was conceiving for the recovery of his lost *jagir*. Such worldly occupations were hateful to Hazrat Mirza Ghulam Ahmad, and he cared nothing for the restoration of the lost dignity and honour of the family. In obedience to his father's wishes, however, he did whatever was required of him. At one time he was compelled to accept Government service at Sialkot, where he passed four years of his life, 1864-1868. His experience in this line of life made upon his heart a deep impression of the degeneracy of those with whom he came in contact in that sphere of action, and therefore he did not mix with them. When his day's work was finished, he would go straight to his residence and bury himself in the pages of his books. Only those who were interested in religion, whether Muslims or non-Muslims, sought his company. It was there that he came in contact with some Christian missionaries, with whom he had conversations on religious topics. Speaking of those days, Maulvi Sirajuddin, the father of Maulvi Zafar Ali Khan, who is one of the greatest opponents of the Ahmadiyya movement, wrote in his paper, the *Zamindar*:

"Mirza Ghulam Ahmad was a clerk in Sialkot about the year 1860 or 1861[5]. His age was then about 22 to 24 years. We can say as an eye-witness that, even in the prime of youth, he was a very righteous and God-fearing man. After finishing his official work, he spent the whole of his time in the study of religious works. He mingled very little with others".

So deep was the impression made upon Maulvi Zafar Ali's father by Hazrat Ahmad's piety and learning that he paid him a visit at Qadian, later in 1877. His impression then, to which, as editor of the *Zamindar*, he subsequently gave expression was still the same:

"In 1877, we had the honour of passing one night as his [Hazrat Ahmad's] guest. In those days, too, he was so deeply devoted to Divine worship and religious study that he did not talk much even with his guests."

At last, his father recalled him from Government service, and he was, for a time, again required to carry on the law-suits relating to his father's estate, but the task was extremely repugnant to him. Even while thus obeying the orders of his father, he devoted a part of his time to the refutation of Christian attacks on Islam. The town of Batala, about eleven miles from Qadian, was an

5. The date is wrong. He joined the service in 1864.

important Christian missionary centre. He
frequented the place in connection with the affairs
of the estate, and it pained him to see how
Christian propaganda, unrefuted as it was, misled
ignorant Muslims. The Batala Muslims, when hard-
pressed by Christian missionaries, would come to
Qadian to seek his help, and he sent them back
well-armed to meet the situation.

Father's death

Mirza Ghulam Murtaza died in June 1876. The
following account of his death is from his son's pen:

"I was told in a vision that the time of my
father's death had drawn nigh. At the time that I
saw this vision, I was at Lahore. I made haste to
reach Qadian and found him very ill, but I never
thought that he would die so soon, for the disease
had abated to an appreciable degree. The next
day we were all sitting by his bedside when, at
noon, he told me to rest for a while, for it was
the month of June and the heat was excessive.
When I lay down for rest, I received the
following revelation: 'By heaven and by the
accident which shall befall after sunset'. I was
given to understand that this revelation was a
kind of condolence from the Almighty, and that
the accident which was to befall was no other
than the death of my father . . . When I received
this revelation foretelling the death of my
father, human weakness made me think that,
since some of the sources of the income of our
family would cease with my father's death, we

might be put in trouble. No sooner had the idea
passed into my mind than I received a second
revelation saying: 'Is God not sufficient for His
servant?' This revelation brought tranquility and
satisfaction to my mind, and went into my heart
like a nail of iron. I call the Lord to witness that
He wrought the fulfilment of the joyful news
contained in this revelation in a wonderful
manner ... My father died that very day after
sunset, and it was the first day in my life that I
saw such a sign of mercy from God [6] ... Thus I
passed about forty years of my life under my
father. His passing away from this life marked
the dawn of a new era for me, and I began to
receive Divine revelations incessantly. I cannot
say what deed of mine drew this grace of God to
me, but I feel that my mind had a natural
attraction for faithfulness to God which no
power in the world could alienate."

RELIGIOUS DEDICATION

Love for the Holy Qur'an

As he himself says, at the age of forty, a new era
thus dawned upon Hazrat Ahmad, and he began to
receive Divine revelations. His father's death
brought about a radical change in his life, and his
religious tendencies began to assume a more
definite form. There was no longer any pressure put
upon him to give himself up to worldly pursuits, and
the whole of his time was from then onwards
devoted to the study of the Holy Qur'an and other

6. This refers to the consoling revelation which he had received.

Islamic literature. He was undoubtedly leading a deeply religious life, but it had taken a quite different course from that which religious devotion normally followed in those days. Many schools of the Muslim Sufis require their votaries to undergo various forms of devotional exercises, of which no indication is found in the practice of the Holy Prophet. Hazrat Ahmad belonged to none of these schools and he never practised such innovations. In fact, from his early life, he hated all ascetic practices which were opposed to the word and the spirit of the Holy Qur'an. His only devotional exercise was the study of the Holy Qur'an in solitude. For days and months, he would continue studying the Holy Book, and so great was his love for it that those who saw him were convinced that he was never tired of reading it. His son, Mirza Sultan Ahmad, who was then a young man of about twenty-five years, bears witness to this in the following words:

"He had a copy of the Holy Qur'an which he was continually reading and marking.[7] I can say without exaggeration that he might have read it ten thousand times."

Divine visions

On one occasion, he saw a vision in which an old man appeared to him saying that, according to the law of prophethood, fasting was a necessary

7. This copy of the Holy Qur'an is now in the possession of the author, and on it, in Hazrat Ahmad's own handwriting, are numbered the Divine commandments and prohibitions contained in the Holy Qur'an.

preparation for receiving Divine light. On the basis of this vision, he kept fasts for a period of eight or nine months, reducing his food during that time to two or three morsels. Nevertheless, he did it privately so as to keep the fact concealed from his nearest relatives, and made special arrangements for the disposal of the food which he received regularly. This long fasting, however, had no injurious effect upon his health. On the other hand, he saw many wonderful visions relating to the future, some of which were later on published in the *Barahin Ahmadiyya*, his first great work. The fulfilment, years afterwards, of the prophecies contained in them showed that they were actual revelations from God and not the hallucinations of a diseased brain.

Anti-Islamic Christian literature

Hazrat Mirza Ghulam Ahmad was, however, no mere visionary. From his early life, he was a student not only of Islam but also of comparative religion. He himself says:

"I have been studying Christian literature from the early age of sixteen or seventeen, and have been pondering over Christian objections. I collected all those objections which the Christians advance against our Holy Prophet [8] . . . Their number is about three thousand. God is a witness and none greater than He can be produced as a witness that, as I have just said, I

8. This collection was accidentally burned later in the life-time of Hazrat Ahmad.

have been studying Christian literature from the time when I was sixteen or seventeen years old, but not for a moment have those objections made any impression on me, or created any doubt in my mind, and this is simply due to the grace of God."

Christianity necessarily attracted his attention first, as that was the only foe of Islam in his early days. We have seen that, during his stay at Sialkot, he had discussions with Christian missionaries about the comparative merits of Islam and Christianity. Returning to Qadian after four years, he actively refuted the anti-Islamic propaganda of Christianity, whose centre was Batala. In fact, Christian propaganda against Islam was most active, and at the same time, most scurrilous, during the latter half of the nineteenth century. Hazrat Mirza Ghulam Ahmad, being a devoted student of religion, closely studied that literature, and his heart ached at the way in which the holiest of men was being maligned and abused. By producing this abusive literature, the aim of Christianity was to engender, in Muslim hearts, hatred for the Holy Founder of Islam. In fact, with its numerous bands of missionaries insinuating themselves into every nook and corner of the Muslim world, and with heaps of abusive literature distributed freely among the Muslims, Christianity was challenging the very existence of Islam, and Hazrat Ahmad, whose heart was full of the deepest conviction of Islamic truth, took up the challenge in real earnest. He started to write against the aggressiveness of Christianity, and articles from his pen began to appear in Muslim periodicals.The publication of such articles in the

Manshur Muhammadi, which was issued from Bangalore in Southern India, shows the keenness with which he was controverting the Christian propaganda.

Comparative study of religion

Hazrat Mirza Ghulam Ahmad was not, however, a mere controversialist. He was a student of religion, and, as early as 1873, while his father was still alive and he was engaged in law-suits relating to the family estates, he had determined to make a comparative study of religion and to place the result of his researches before the public. He had already decided to write a book, and the following memorandum in his own handwriting shows his deep consciousness of the superiority and the perfection of the Islamic teachings which it had become his life's aim to establish and for which he wanted freedom from worldly entanglements:

"In this book, it will be necessary to state that the law of Mustafa [the Islamic Law] is perfect and more comprehensive than all other laws. To prove this, a law shall be taken for example from the Torah in the first place, then from the Gospels, and after that from the Holy Qur'an, so that when the reader compares the three laws, it will be evident to him which of the three laws is the best and the excellent."

This note is signed thus: "Ghulam Ahmad, 17th Oct. 1873, Friday, Qadian."

The Arya Samaj

He was preparing himself for this great work by studying not only the Islamic literature, the Holy Qur'an, Hadith and commentaries, but also the literature of other religions, in his spare time. His father's death, in 1876, had opened the way for him to realize the great dream of his life - to establish the superiority of Islam over all other religions. While he was thus fighting single-handed against the vast forces of Christianity, another foe of Islam had appeared in the field, in the form of the Arya Samaj. The founder of this new off-shoot of Hinduism was born in distant Kathiawar, Gujerat, in the Bombay Presidency, in the year 1824. At an early age he fled from his home, and after visiting various centres of Hindu learning and formally starting his mission in 1875, at Bombay, he gave final shape to it two years later, at Lahore, the capital of the Punjab, and the Arya Samaj of today rests on the principles enunciated there. Originally, this movement was directed against the idol-worship of Hinduism, but, as Western education was opening the Hindu mind for the acceptance of Christianity and Islam, the Arya Samaj, from its inception, came into conflict with these two religions.

The Punjab proved to be a fertile land for the Arya Samaj, and, by the end of the year 1878, branches of the organization were established all over the Punjab, one being established at Qadian itself. It was through this local branch that Hazrat Ahmad was drawn into a controversy with the Arya Samaj. The local discussion soon assumed importance and found its way into the columns of both Hindu and Muslim papers of Lahore and Amritsar. The *Hindu Bandhu* of Lahore, which was edited by Pandit Shiv Narain Agni Hotri, who later became the founder of another Hindu sect, called the Dev Samaj, opened its columns to articles for and against the Arya Samaj.

The following note from a Hindu editor's pen shows how powerfully Hazrat Ahmad was carrying the fight against the Arya Samaj:

"Our readers will remember that the final paper of Mirza Ghulam Ahmad sahib which we published in our issue for February, 1879, could not be produced in its entirety in the said number, and was therefore completed in the two following numbers. In that article, the Mirza sahib also made an announcement in which he addressed Swami Dayanand, the founder of the Arya Samaj, as well as some of his followers (whose names were given in the said number for February, 1879, on p. 39) We very gladly gave room to that article in our periodical and we entertained the hope that, if the arguments given by the Mirza sahib, which were very *clear and based on logical principles, were appreciated by the above mentioned gentlemen,* [9] they would, according to their declared principle that one should always be ready to accept the truth and to give up untruth, publicly and openly declare their faith

9. Italics are mine - *author.*

in the falsity of the transmigration of souls, and thus establish an example of their willingness to accept the truth."

The Brahmo Samaj

It has elsewhere been shown that Hazrat Ahmad had studied the Bible. His controversies with the Arya Samajists show that he had also studied the Vedas, from such translations as were available, and he repeatedly called upon his opponents to judge the merits of the Holy Qur'an as compared with other sacred books. Not only was he a student of comparative religion, but he also claimed to have the religious experience which makes men attain communion with God. Therefore it was that he had to devote much of his attention to the Brahmo Samaj, an earlier Hindu reform movement, started by Ram Mohan Roy in 1828. It is a well-established fact that the founder of the Brahmo Samaj was mainly influenced by the Muslim Sufi ideals. It was thus a very liberal movement, based on the principle that all religions are true. Yet, strangely enough, it denied the possibility of revelation, and it was this aspect of the Brahmo Samaj which attracted the attention of Hazrat Ahmad. Pandit Shiv Narain Agni Hotri, the great Brahmo leader at Lahore, himself carried on this controversy, but, after some time, he deserted the Brahmo Samaj and laid the foundation of a new sect, called the Dev Samaj.

MUJADDID OF THE FOURTEENTH CENTURY

Claim as Mujaddid

As I have already stated, Hazrat Ahmad was not a mere controversialist. He was a student of religion who had made a close study of Islam as well as of other religions and had come to the conclusion that, while other religions contained only partial truth, Islam contained the whole truth, and was, on account of this superiority, destined to be the future religion of the world. To establish this fact he began to write a book called the *Barahin Ahmadiyya*, the full name being *Al-Barahin al-Ahmadiyya 'ala haqqiyyat-i-Kitab Allah al-Qur'an wal-nubuwwat-il-Muhammadiyya*, i.e., "The Ahmadiyya proofs for the truth of the Book of God, the Qur'an, and the prophethood of Muhammad".

Two years later, i.e., in the closing year of the thirteenth century of Hijra, he issued a third part of the same book, in which were published several revelations which he had received from God, in one of which he claimed to be the promised reformer, *mujaddid*, of the fourteenth century of Hijra. This revelation, which is published on page 238 of the book, runs thus:

"The Beneficent God has taught thee the Qur'an so that thou mayest warn a people whose fathers have not been warned, and so that the erroneous path of the guilty may be seen manifestly. Say, I have been commanded by God to deliver His message and I have been commanded by God to deliver His message and I am the first of believers."

At the same time he issued a manifesto stating plainly that he was the *mujaddid* of that century. In this manifesto, he wrote, after speaking of this book:

"This servant of Allah has given a manifest proof by the grace of God the Almighty that many of the true inspirations and signs and minor miracles and news relating to the unseen and Divine secrets and the visions and prayers that have been accepted are a part of the religious experience of this servant of the faith, the truth of these being borne witness to by many of the religious opponents [the Aryas and others]. All these matters have been related in this book, and the author has been given the knowledge *that he is the* mujaddid *of this time* and that spiritually his excellences resemble the excellences of Messiah, the son of Mary, and that the one of them bears a very strong resemblance and a close relation to the other."

At that time, the Muslims highly appreciated the great services which Hazrat Ahmad had rendered to the cause of Islam, and greatly admired not only his learning and his powerful refutation of the opponents of Islam, but also his righteousness and piety, and, therefore, they hailed these claims as quite opportune. It was just the commencement of the fourteenth century of Hijra, and a hadith of the Holy Prophet promised to them a reformer at the commencement of each century. Besides the hadith,

the condition of things in the world of Islam called
yet more loudly for the appearance of a reformer.
Islam was at the time between two fires – disputes
and dissensions which frittered away the whole
energy of the Muslim world, and the most terrible
attacks on it from without. Here was a man who
rose far above all internal dissensions, refusing to
take part in them, and who directed his attention
solely to the attacks from without; a soldier of
Islam who championed the cause of Islam most
powerfully, meeting every opponent on his own
ground; a learned man whose exposition of the Holy
Qur'an exactly met the need of the time; the fame
of his piety was spread far and wide; and what more
was needed for a reformer? His claim to be the
mujaddid was, therefore, generally accepted by the
Muslims, laymen as well as theologians.

An epoch-making book

Two years later, in 1884, came out the fourth
part of the *Barahin Ahmadiyya*, which contained a
most powerful exposition of the truth of Islam. This
book may rightly be regarded as marking a new
epoch in the religious literature of Islam, and it
was accorded that position by the greatest *'ulama*
of the time. Its real object was to establish the
Truth of Islam by a long series of cogent and
irrefutable reasons and arguments, but by way of
comparison dogmas of other religions were also
included and subjected to the search-light of
reason, and thus the beauties of Islam were
manifested all the more clearly. Even such a hostile
critic as Walter admits that "this book was quite

universally acclaimed (in so far as it was read), throughout the Muhammadan world as a work of power and originality".[10] The book won this recognition in spite of the fact that it contained all the material which formed the basis of later differences with the orthodox Muslims. In this work were published the author's revelations in which he was addressed as messenger, prophet and warner. His claim to be inspired by God was never contested. Thus, Maulvi Muhammad Husain, the head of the *Ahl Hadith* (Wahabi) sect in the Punjab, wrote a review of the *Barahin Ahmadiyya*, and the following paragraph from this review shows how wide was the acceptance accorded to this book by men of all shades of opinion, the author being a declared Hanafi, to which school of thought he adhered to the last:

"In our opinion, it is in this time and in the present circumstances, a book the like of which has not been written up to this time in Islam, and nothing can be said about the future; Allah may bring about another affair after this. Its author, too, has proved himself firm in helping the cause of Islam, with his property and his person and his pen and his tongue and his personal religious experience, to such an extent that an example of it is rarely met with among the Muslims who have gone before. If any one looks upon these words of ours as an Asiatic exaggeration, let him point out to us at least one such book as has in it such forceful refutation of all classes of the opponents of Islam, especially the Arya Samaj

10. H. A. Walter, *The Ahmadiyya Movement*, p. 16.

and the Brahmo Samaj, and let him give us the addresses of two or three persons, the helpers of the cause of Islam, who, besides helping Islam with their properties and their persons and their pens and their tongues, have also come forward with their religious experience and have proclaimed, as against the opponents of Islam and the deniers of revelation, the manly challenge that whoever doubted the truth of revelation may come to them and witness the truth thereof, and who have made non-Muslims taste of the same." [11]

Religious experience

Muslims of the *Ahl Sunna wal-Jama'a* sect generally admit the existence of saints, or *auliya Allah*, who have been recipients of the gifts of Divine inspiration, while the *Ahl Hadith*, popularly known as Wahabis, are generally looked upon as denying the continuance of this gift; nevertheless, here we find the head of the *Ahl Hadith* sect, not only admiring the powerful arguments contained in the *Barahin Ahmadiyya* against all sorts of opponents of Islam but also laying special stress on the fact that the author's religious experience was of such a high character, in holding communion with God and in receiving inspiration or revelation from Him, that he had been successful in giving practical proof of such revelation to its deniers. This is only one indication of how Muslim India received Hazrat Mirza Ghulam Ahmad's claim as *mujaddid* of the fourteenth century of Hijra. The purpose of his

11. *Isha'at al-Sunna*, vol. vii, June to November, 1884, p. 157.

being raised as a *mujaddid* was also made clear in the *Barahin Ahmadiyya*. I quote Hazrat Ahmad's own words:

"The spiritual triumph of the religion of Islam which would be brought about by conclusive arguments and shining proofs is destined to be accomplished through this weak mortal, whether it is in his life-time or after his death. Though the religion of Islam has been triumphant from the beginning on account of its truthful arguments, and though from the earliest times its opponents have met with disgrace and dishonour, its conquests over the different sects and nations depended on the coming of a time which, by opening the ways of communication, should turn the whole world into a kind of united states . . . Thus God intends, by creating me in this age and by granting me hundreds of heavenly signs and extraordinary matters relating to the future, and deep knowledge and truths, and by giving me knowledge of hundreds of sure arguments, to spread and propagate knowledge of the true teachings of the Qur'an among all nations and in all countries." [12]

Bai'a to serve Islam

Matters remained in this condition for several years during which time Hazrat Mirza Ghulam Ahmad was generally admitted to be the religious leader and inspired reformer of the Muslims. During that time, he maintained a hard struggle against the

12. *Barahin Ahmadiyya*, pp. 498-502.

onslaughts of the Arya Samaj, which had become very powerful, and which followed in the footsteps of the Christian missionaries in abusing the Prophet of Islam. On the first of December, 1888, he announced that Almighty God had commanded him to accept *bai'a* and to form into a separate class those who came to spiritual life through him.

"I have been commanded", he wrote, "that those who seek after truth should enter my *bai'a*, in order to give up dirty habits and slothful and disloyal ways of life and in order to imbibe true faith and a truly pure life that springs from faith and to learn the ways of the love of God".

Bai'a is, among the Sufis, the oath of fealty which the disciple takes when giving his hand into the hand of his spiritual guide, but the *bai'a* which Hazrat Ahmad wanted from his followers was a promise to guard the cause of Islam, to deliver the message thereof, and to place the service of Islam above all other considerations. There were ten conditions which the disciple had to accept, the eighth of these being:

"That he will regard religion and the honour of religion and the sympathy of Islam as dearer to him than his life and his property and his honour and his children and every one dear to him."

These ten conditions were retained after his claim to the Promised Messiahship and up to the end of his life, but when disciples came in larger numbers, these were shortened, the following words taking the place of the eighth condition:

"I will place religion above the world".

It is easy to see that this pledge was quite different from the ordinary pledge which is taken in the Sufi orders, and its object was no other than to uphold the honour of Islam at all costs, to guard Islam against all attacks and to carry its message to the farthest ends of the world. Here was a spiritual commander who needed a spiritual force to guard the spiritual territories of Islam and to lead Islam to further spiritual conquests.

MAHDI AND MESSIAH

Claim to Messiahship

The task before him was a difficult one. The Muslims had lost that love and zeal for the spread of Islam which led the earlier sons of Islam to the distant corners of the world. Many people, however, came to him and took the pledge. While preparing himself and his followers for the great conquests, he made an announcement which fell like a bombshell among the Muslim public - that Jesus Christ was not alive, as was generally believed by the Muslims, but that he had died as all other prophets had died, and that his advent among the Muslims meant the advent of a *mujaddid* in his spirit and power; that no Mahdi would come, as generally thought, to convert unbelievers with the sword, as this was opposed to the basic teachings of the Qur'an, but that the Mahdi's conquests were to be spiritual; and that the prophecies relating to the advent of a Messiah and a Mahdi were fulfilled in his own person. It was about eighteen months after his call to *bai'a* that this announcement was made and it changed the whole attitude of the Muslim community towards him. Those very people who hailed him in his capacity of *mujaddid* as the saviour of Islam now called him an impostor, an arch-heretic and Anti-Christ.

Recluse and soldier

Hazrat Ahmad based both his claims, the claim to mujaddidship and the claim to Messiahship, on Divine revelation, and it is easy to see that nothing but the fullest conviction that he was commanded by God could have led him to adopt a course which, he knew, would bring him from the height of fame and distinction, to which he had attained, to the depth of degradation in the eyes of his own community. If public esteem and fame were the goal of Hazrat Ahmad's aspirations, he had indeed achieved them. He knew that his departure from an established popular conception must injure his reputation and turn his very friends and admirers into foes; but he cared little for public opinion and even less for fame. He was then an old man and the fifty-five years of his earlier life show but one desire – the desire to see Islam triumphant in the world – and they point to but one aim – the aim to serve the cause of Islam. His father had often remonstrated with him on account of his neglect of his worldly concerns and had exhorted him to look after the family estate, but in vain. He had not shown the least desire to become a great man in the world; he did not even care to maintain the position which his family enjoyed. His love of solitude continued unabated to the last and the only thing for which he would come in contact with others was to uphold the dignity of Islam and to safeguard its honour. He was a recluse all his life, except when duty called him to fight the battle of Islam, and then he was a soldier who could wield his weapon against each and every assailant. The stream of life which had flowed consistently and constantly in one direction could not suddenly take a turn in the opposite direction. The hand of God had undoubtedly been preparing him from early life to champion the cause of Islam, and he was at this point Divinely directed to remove, by his claim to Promised Messiahship and Mahdiship, the two great obstacles which stood in the way of the propagation of Islam.

Today any one can see that Islam and Christianity are the only two religions contending for the spiritual mastery of the world, all other religions being limited to one or two countries. At the time when the Promised Messiah began to work, Islam seemed to have been utterly vanquished by Christianity, not only by reason of the temporal ascendancy of Christianity but also because Christianity was completely master in the field of propaganda, Islam being almost entirely unrepresented. In this helpless state, the Muslims had, to a very great extent, come under the influence of the Christian propaganda, which, on the one hand, impugned the character of the Holy Prophet, and, on the other, laid stress on the superiority of Jesus Christ over the Founder of Islam. In support of this latter allegation were

brought forward certain erroneous views which had
taken root among the Muslims; for instance, that
Jesus Christ was alive in the heavens while all the
other prophets had died, and that he would reappear
in the world when Islam would be in great distress,
and thus that he would, in the real sense, be the
last Prophet and the saviour of Islam. To establish
the superiority of Islam and to open the way for its
conquest of the world, it was necessary not only to
clear the character of the Holy Prophet of those
false charges but also to uproot those erroneous
doctrines. Thus, when Hazrat Mirza Ghulam Ahmad
was commissioned for the great task of leading
Islam to a world-conquest, when the Divine mantle
of mujaddidship fell upon his shoulders and when he
began to enlist, through *bai'a*, an army of soldiers
to fight the spiritual battle of Islam, God gave him
the knowledge that the prevailing view of the
Muslim world relating to Jesus Christ was erroneous
and not supported by the Holy Qur'an, that Jesus
Christ had died as had all other prophets and that
his prophesied second advent was to be taken in a
metaphorical sense and to mean the advent of a
reformer (*mujaddid*) with his spirit and power.

Two baseless doctrines

The two matters were so closely correlated that
in the solution of the one lay the solution of the
other. If Jesus was dead, his personal second advent
was impossible, and that prophecy could be
interpreted only in the same way as Jesus himself
interpreted the prophecy of the second advent of
Elijah. The false conception that Jesus was alive in

heaven was, however, so deep-rooted in the Muslim mind that they would listen to no arguments which militated against this long- cherished belief, even though they were based on the absolute authority of the Holy Qur'an and the Hadith. They were not in a mood to think that, in the very fitness of things, this exactly should be the mission of the *mujaddid* of this age. Christianity, practically the only adversary of Islam and the most formidable, had this one main prop to support its whole structure of doctrines and dogmas - Jesus sitting with God in heaven. To pull this main prop down would mean the crumbling of the whole like a house of cards, and this work had to be done to open the way for the conquests of Islam in the West.

Coupled with the wrong notion that Jesus Christ was alive in heaven and would come down, there was another equally unfounded conception, and equally detrimental to the cause of Islam, namely that the Mahdi would appear just at the same time and would wage war to enforce Islam at the point of sword. Already Islam had been misrepresented in the West as having been estabished by means of the sword, and the doctrine of a Mahdi coming to wage war to establish the superiority of Islam only lent further support to the misrepresentations of the Christian West, causing the hatred against Islam to become deeper and deeper day by day. That false notion also had to be cut at the very roots. "There is no compulsion in religion" (2:256), was a clear principle established by the Holy Qur'an, and there was not a single instance in which the Holy Prophet brought the pressure of the sword to bear on any one individual, let alone a whole nation, to compel the embracing of Islam. "Fight against those who fight against you" (2:190), was the only permission that Islam gave in the matter of fighting, and even the Holy Prophet, to say nothing of the Mahdi, could not go against the Holy Qur'an. The Mahdi (lit., *the guided one*), was only another name for the Messiah – such was the announcement made by Hazrat Ahmad, and in support of this was quoted the Prophet's hadith: "There is no Mahdi but the Messiah."[13]

Storm of opposition

Hazrat Mirza Ghulam Ahmad had thus, in the very cause of Islam, to combat the idea that, for its conquests, Islam stood in need either of Jesus Christ or the sword. He emphasized that men endowed with great gifts, even men like the Messiah, could rise among its followers, and that the spiritual power of Islam was greater than all the swords of the world; but Mulla mentality was too narrow for these broad views. Led by Maulvi Muhammad Husain, the *Ahl Hadith* leader, who had only six years before acclaimed Hazrat Ahmad as one of the greatest sons of Islam, and as one who had rendered unique service to the cause of Islam by his powerful arguments and by the heavenly signs which he had shown to his opponents, the *'ulama* now declared him to be an arch-heretic. Some of them even went so far as to declare that he and his followers could not enter mosques or be buried in Muslim graveyards, that their property could be taken away with impunity and that their marriages

13. *Ibn Majah, Ch. Shiddat al-Zaman.*

were void. The storm of opposition that followed those *fatwas* can better be imagined than described, but all this opposition did not make Hazrat Ahmad swerve an inch from the position which he had taken. The most hostile critics have nothing but praise for his courage in the face of the bitterest opposition, even of attempts at physical violence. Thus wrote Dr Griswold:

"His persistency in affirming his claims in the face of the most intense and bitter opposition is magnificent. He is willing to suffer on behalf of his claims." [14]

Resolution to carry Islam forward

As I have stated, the opposition came not from one quarter but from all sides. All sects of Islam denounced him, just as they had all praised him before, while the Christians and the Arya Samajists, against whom he had been fighting in the cause of Islam for so long a time, were only too glad to join hands with the Muslims. In spite of all, Hazrat Ahmad stood adamant. No abuse, no denunciation, no persecution, no threat of murder disturbed for a single moment the equilibrium of his mind or caused him to entertain for an instant the idea of relinquishing in despair the cause which he had so long upheld. Nay, in the midst of a widespread and bitter opposition on all sides, he reaffirmed with still greater force his resolution to carry the message of Islam to the farthest ends of the world, and his conviction that Islam would triumph became

14. H. A. Walter, *The Ahmadiyya Movement*, p. 21.

greater. It is the unique spectacle of a soldier carrying on the fight single-handed while the powerful forces of opposition were arrayed before his face, and he was being hit in the back by the very people for whom he was fighting. The claim to Promised Messiahship was advanced in three books which appeared one after another at short intervals. In the first of these he writes:

"Do not wonder that Almighty God has in this time of need and in the days of this deep darkness sent down a heavenly light and, having chosen a servant of His for the good of mankind in general, He has sent him to make uppermost the religion of Islam and to spread the light brought by the best of His creatures [15] and to strengthen the cause of the Muslims and to purify their internal condition." [16]

And again:

"And the truth will win and the freshness and light of Islam which characterized it in the earlier days will be restored and that sun will rise again as it arose first in the full resplendence of its light. But it is necessary that heaven should withold its rising till our hearts bleed with labour and hard work and we sacrifice all comforts for its appearance and submit ourselves to all kinds of disgrace for the honour of Islam. The life of Islam demands a sacrifice

15. This refers to the Holy Prophet Muhammad.
16. *Fath Islam*, p. 7.

from us, and what is that? That we die in this way." [17]

Significance underlying claim

Apart from the narrow-minded Mulla who could not grasp the significance underlying Hazrat Ahmad's claim to Promised Messiahship, even the educated Muslim thinks that this claim brought nothing but schism in the house of Islam. It is true that much of Hazrat Ahmad's time was taken up, after 1891, with controversy against the orthodox, and it became bitter too at times, but the internal struggle never made him lose sight of his real objective, which had indeed become more marked and definite. As to internal dissensions, they were already there; in fact, the Muslims had lost all objectives except fighting amongst themselves on the minutest points of difference. Therefore, they had no eye for the higher issues involved in Hazrat Ahmad's claim, but spent their whole force in carrying on a struggle about minor differences. Moreover, the great cause of Islam - its onward march in the world - had nothing to lose from the claim to Promised Messiahship; Jesus' death added only one more to the numerous prophets who, including the Holy Prophet Muhammad, had all died; but to Christianity it meant the death of its central figure, with whose death collapsed the whole structure of its dogmas. Nay, the cause of Islam gained immeasurable strength therefrom; for, as long as the Muslim believed that Jesus was alive in heaven and that he would make his descent at some

17. *Fath Islam,* p. 16.

future time to bring about the triumph of Islam, his
mentality remained one of fond dreams never to be
realized, and that was largely the reason why the
Muslim had lost the zeal and energy of the earlier
days for carrying forward the message of Islam.
Islam's triumph was, he believed, bound up with the
coming of Jesus Christ and of Imam Mahdi, and he
had nothing to do but to wait and see. Such was the
hidden process of thought which made him quite
inactive. That the Messiah who was to come had
already appeared was an idea which shifted the
responsibility to his own shoulders; nay, it brought
back to him the zeal to carry forward the message
of Islam. If the Messiah had come, the time had also
arrived for the world conquest of Islam. This was
the great mental revolution achieved among those
who accepted Hazrat Ahmad as the Messiah; a mere
handful of men, but carrying the message of Islam
to the farthest ends of the world, while the millions
of the orthodox are either idle or occupied with
their internal dissensions.

From defence to attack

In Hazrat Mirza Ghulam Ahmad's own work, two
changes are clearly witnessed with his claim to
Promised Messiahship. The first is that, as far as
the contest with Christianity was concerned, he had
hitherto been carrying on a defensive war –
clearing the Holy Prophet of the false charges
brought against him by the Christian missionaries;
but his new claim involved an aggressive line of
action – the destruction of the very foundations on
which the Church, as distinguished from the

Christianity preached by Christ, was built. Right at the beginning of *Fath Islam*, his first pamphlet making the new announcement, he wrote clearly:

"I . . . bear a strong resemblance to the nature of the Messiah, and it is owing to this natural resemblance that I have been sent in the name of the Messiah, so that the doctrine of the cross may be shattered to pieces. Therefore, I have been sent to break the cross and to kill the swine" (p. 17).

Thus the contest between Christianity and Islam was no longer to be limited to the defence of Islam; the spiritual forces of Islam had to be gathered together to attack Christianity itself.

Dajjal and Gog and Magog

The other change which resulted from the claim to Promised Messiahship was that it gave a definite direction to the mission which Hazrat Ahmad believed had been entrusted to him, namely to bring about the triumph of Islam and to lead it on to a world-conquest. Henceforth, Europe or the Western world became his special objective, and that new idea was born as a twin to the idea that he was the Promised Messiah. Both ideas - the idea that he was the Promised Messiah and the idea that his mission was to carry the message of Islam to the Western world - took their birth at one and the same time. It was not a casual coincidence; the two ideas were closely interrelated. The advent of the Promised Messiah did not stand alone in eschatological

prophecy; it was essentially combined with the idea
of the appearance of the Anti-Christ (*Dajjal*) and
of Gog and Magog (*Ya'juj wa Ma'juj*). In fact, the
Promised Messiah's first and foremost work was to
be to put an end to the influence of the *Dajjal* and
of Gog and Magog. Now the prevalent idea among
the Muslims was that the *Dajjal* was a one-eyed man
who would make his appearance in the latter days
with the treasures of the world at his command,
that he would lay claim to Godhead, carrying even
paradise and hell with him, and that he would
traverse the whole earth in forty days, visiting
every habitation of men, inviting them to accept his
divinity and enriching those who followed him, and
that Gog and Magog would be an extraordinary
creation of God, who would spread over the whole
earth. The truth, which had remained hidden for
thirteen centuries after the Holy Prophet
Muhammad, flashed upon Hazrat Ahmad's mind at
the very time when he was raised to the dignity of
Messiahship. This truth was that the *Dajjal* and Gog
and Magog of the prophecies were no other than the
Christian nations of Europe and America. In their
religious attitude, in contradicting the teachings of
Christ and the teachings of all the prophets of God,
they represented Gog and Magog. Thus, when
announcing his claim to Promised Messiahship, after
discussing at length the prophecies relating to their
appearance, he wrote in *Izala Auham*, his first
great work on the subject, under the caption, *It was
necessary that the Anti-Christ should come forth
from the Church*:

"Now this question deserves to be solved that, as

the advent of the Messiah, the son of Mary, is meant for the *Dajjal*, if I have come in the spirit of the Messiah, who is the *Dajjal* against me? . . . In the first place, it must be remembered that literally *Dajjal* means *an association of liars who mix up truth with falsehood and who use deceit and underhand means to lead astray the creation of God* . . . If we ponder over . . . the condition of all those people who have done the work of *Dajjal* since the creation of Adam, we do not find another people who have manifested that characteristic to the extent to which the Christian missionaries have done. They have before their eyes an imaginary Messiah who, they allege, is still living and who claimed to be God; but the Messiah, son of Mary, never claimed to be God; it is they who are claiming Divinity on his behalf, and to make this claim successful, they have resorted to all kinds of alterations and have made use of all means of deceit. With the exception of Makka and Madina, there is no place to which they have not gone . . . They are so rich that the treasures of the world go along with them wherever they go . . . And they carry along with them a kind of paradise and hell. So, whoever is willing to accept their religion, that paradise is shown to him, and whoever becomes a severe opponent of them, he is threatened with hell . . . There is not one sign of the *Dajjal* that is not met with in them . . . Hence those people represent the *Dajjal* who has come forth from the Church.

"Now doubts are raised that the *Dajjal* must be one-eyed, being blind in the right eye, that Gog and Magog must appear at the same time . . . and that the sun must arise from the west at the same time . . .

"These doubts would vanish when it is seen that *one-eyed* does not mean physically blind in one eye. God says in the Holy Qur'an: 'Whoever is blind in this life shall be blind in the hereafter'. Does 'the blind' here carry the significance of physical blindness? Nay, it means spiritual blindness. And the meaning is that the *Dajjal* shall be devoid of spiritual wisdom, and that, though he will make great inventions and show great wonders as if he were claiming Godhead, yet he will have no spiritual eye, just as we find today is the case with the people of Europe and America that they have gone to the utmost extent in worldly scheming.

"As regards Gog and Magog, it is unquestionable that these are two prosperous nations of the world, one of them being the English (Teuton) and the other the Russians (Slavs). Both these nations are directing their attacks from a height towards what is beneath their feet, i.e., they are becoming victorious with their God-given powers . . . Both these nations are also mentioned in the Bible.

"As regards the rising of the sun from the West, we do believe in it; but what has been shown to me in a vision is this - that the rising of the sun from the West signifies that the Western world which has been involved of old in the darkness of unbelief and error shall be made to shine with the sun of Truth, and those people shall have their share of Islam. I saw that I was standing on a pulpit in the city of London and explaining the truth of Islam in a strongly-argumented speech in the English language; and, after this, I caught a large number of birds that were sitting on small trees, and in colour they were white, and their size was probably the size of the partridge. So I intepreted this dream as meaning that, though I may not personally go there, yet my writings would spread among those people and many righteous Englishmen would accept the truth. In reality, the Western countries have, up to this time, shown very little aptitude for religious truths, as if spiritual wisdom had in its entirety been granted to Asia, and material wisdom to Europe and America ... now Almighty God intends to cast on them the look of mercy."[18]

Islamization of Europe

One wonders when one finds that a man who lived in a village, far removed from all centres of activity, who did not know a word of English, whose knowledge of Europe was almost negligible, has visions that he is delivering a speech in English in London and explaining the truths of Islam to Europeans, and that the people of Europe will accept Islam. The history of Islam shows how such visions have materialized before. The great saint of Ajmer, Khwaja Mu'in al-Din Chishti, saw in a dream, while in Madina, that he was preaching Islam in India, and the saint of Qadian sees in a vision that he is spreading Islam in Europe. India has

18. *Izala Auham*, pp. 478-516.

fulfilled the dream of the saint of Ajmer, and Europe is undoubtedly on its way to fulfil the vision of the saint of Qadian.

Amidst all the persecution to which he was subjected, Hazrat Ahmad's heart throbbed with but one desire - the desire to spread Islam in the West - and that was the message with which he came as the Promised Messiah. Europe was identical with *Dajjal*, and the Messiah must overcome the *Dajjal*. Flames of the fire of opposition rose high on all sides, but he had an eye on the goal and he proposed to sit down calmly in the midst of this fire and write books disclosing the beauties of Islam and meeting the objections not only of Christian missionaries but also of those whom materialism was bringing in its train:

"Then so far as it lies in my power I intend to broadcast, in all the countries of Europe and Asia, the knowledge and blessings which the Holy Spirit of God has granted me ... It is undoubtedly true that Europe and America have a large collection of objections against Islam, inculcated through those engaged in Mission work, and that their philosophy and natural sciences give rise to another sort of criticism. My enquiries have led me to the conclusion that there are nearly three thousand points which have been raised as objections against Islam ... To meet these objections, a chosen man is needed who should have a river of knowledge flowing in his vast breast and whose knowledge should have been specially broadened and deepened by Divine inspiration ... So my advice is that ... writings of a good type should be sent into these countries. If my people help me heart and soul I wish to prepare a commentary of the Holy Qur'an which should be sent to them after it has been rendered into the English language. I cannot refrain from stating clearly that this is my work, and that no one else can do it as well as I or he who is an offshoot of mine and thus is included in me."[19]

"In this critical time, a man has been raised up by God and he desires that he may show the beautiful face of Islam to the whole world and open its ways to the Western countries."[20]

OPPOSITION

Controversies with 'Ulama

Though his real objective was the spread of Islam in the West, he could not avoid controversy with the orthodox 'ulama who opposed him tooth and nail. Often he would say that, if the 'ulama left him alone, he would devote himself, heart and soul, to the cause of the advancement of Islam, but he had perforce to write a large number of books, tracts and pamphlets to explain his own position, and to carry on a number of controversies. The first controversy took place at Ludhiana, soon after the announcement of his claim to Promised Messiahship, with Maulvi Muhammad Husain of Batala, his erstwhile admirer, and lasted from 20th to 29th

19. *Izala Auham*, pp. 771-773.
20. *Op. cit.*, p. 769.

July, 1891. Particulars of this controversy are contained in a pamphlet called *al-Haqq*. From Ludhiana he went to Delhi, the great stronghold of orthodox *'ulama*, and there he met with the severest opposition. As far as the claim itself was concerned, there was nothing in it that could be called heretical. Every Muslim had a right to interpret the Qur'an and the Hadith, and Hazrat Mirza Ghulam Ahmad did not for a moment deny those authorities, but put on them an interpretation different from that which the orthodox Mullas held, and on that score, no one could find fault with him. He again and again explained that the Holy Qur'an repeatedly spoke of the death of Jesus Christ and did not, on a single occasion, state that he was alive in heaven or that he was raised up bodily to some upper region. Therefore, his advent, as spoken of in Hadith, could be taken only in a metaphorical sense, and the claim to Promised Messiahship was only an offshoot of his generally recognized claim to mujaddidship. The *'ulama* could not meet him on that ground - the position was so clear - and therefore they resorted to misrepresentations, saying that he denied certain articles of the Muslim faith; for instance, that he claimed to be a prophet, and thus denied the finality of the prophethood of the Holy Prophet Muhammad, that he denied the existence of angels, that he denied miracles and so on.

Refutation of false charges

These charges were refuted by him again and again. The following manifesto was issued by him at

Delhi on 2nd October, 1891. It is headed, *An Announcement by a Traveller*, and opens thus:

"I have heard that some of the leading *'ulama* of this city are giving publicity to the false charge against me that I lay claim to prophethood and that I do not believe in angels, or in heaven and hell, or in the existence of Gabriel, or in *Lailat al-Qadr*, or in miracles and the Mi'raj of the Holy Prophet. So, in the interest of truth, I do hereby publicly declare that all this is complete fabrication. I am not a claimant to prophethood, neither am I a denier of miracles, angels, *Lailat al-Qadr*, etc. On the other hand, I confess belief in all those matters which are included in the Islamic principles of faith, and, in accordance with the belief of *Ahl Sunna wal Jama'a*, I believe in all those things which are established by the Qur'an and Hadith, and I believe that any claimant to prophethood and apostleship after our lord and master Muhammad Mustafa (may peace and the blessings of God be upon him), the last of the apostles, is a liar and an unbeliever. It is my conviction that Divine revelation, which is granted to apostles, began with Adam, the chosen one of God, and came to a close with the Apostle of God, Muhammad Mustafa (may peace and the blessings of God be upon him)."

A few days later, he addressed an assembly in the Jami' Masjid of Delhi in the following words:

"Other charges which are advanced against me that I am a denier of *Lailat al-Qadr*, miracles and Mi'raj, and that I am also a claimant to prophethood and a denier of the finality of prophethood - all these charges are untrue and absolutely false. In all these matters, my belief is the same as the belief of other *Ahl Sunna wal Jama'a* and such objections against my books, *Tauzih Maram* and *Izala Auham*, are only an error of the fault-finders. Now I make a plain confession of the following matters, before the Muslims in this house of God - I am a believer in the finality of the prophethood of the Last of the Prophets (may peace and the blessings of God be upon him) and I look upon anyone who denies the finality of the prophethood to be a heretic and outside the pale of Islam. Similarly, I am a believer in angels, miracles, etc."

No claim to prophethood

It is rather strange that he was charged as laying claim to prophethood in his book *Izala Auham*, which contains a large number of statements expressly denying a claim to prophethood and expressing faith in the finality of the prophethood of Muhammad. I refer here to only one such statement, which is given in the form of question and answer:

"*Question*: In the pamphlet *Fath Islam*, claim has been laid to prophethood.

"*Answer*: There is no claim to being a prophet but a claim to being a *muhaddath* (one who is spoken to by God, though not a prophet), and this claim has been advanced by the command of Allah. Further, there is also no doubt that *muhaddathiyya* also contains a strong part of prophethood ... If then this be called metaphorically prophethood or be regarded as a strong part of prophethood, does this amount to a claim to prophethood?" (pp. 421, 422)

Early in the following year, he went to Lahore, where he held a controversy with Maulvi 'Abd al-Hakim. That controversy was brought to a close by the following announcement which Hazrat Ahmad made in the presence of several witnesses:

"Be it known to all the Muslims that all such words as occur in my writings *Fath Islam, Tauzih Maram* and *Izala Auham*, to the effect that the *muhaddath* is in one sense a prophet, or that *muhaddathiyya* is partial prophethood or imperfect prophethood, are not to be taken in the real sense, but have been used according to their root-meaning; otherwise, I lay no claim whatever to actual prophethood. On the other hand, as I have written in my book *Izala Auham*, p. 137, my belief is that our lord and master Muhammad Mustafa (may peace and the blessings of God be upon him) is the last of the prophets. So I wish to make it known to all Muslims that, if they are displeased with these words and if these words give injury to their feelings, they may regard all such words as amended and may read instead the word *muhaddath*, for I do by no means wish to create any dissension among the Muslims. From the beginning, as God knows best, my intention

has never been to use this word *nabi* as meaning
actually a prophet, but only as signifying
muhaddath, which the Holy Prophet has explained
as meaning *one who is spoken to by God*. Of the
muhaddath it is stated in a saying of the Holy
Prophet: 'Among those that were before you of
the Israelites, there used to be men who were
spoken to by God, though they were not prophets,
and if there is one among my followers, it is
'Umar' (*Bukhari*). Therefore, I have not the least
hesitation in stating my meaning in another form
for the conciliation of my Muslim brethren, and
that other form is that wherever the word *nabi*
(prophet) is used in my writings, it should be
taken as meaning *muhaddath*, and the word *nabi*
should be regarded as having been blotted out."

This writing was drawn up in the form of an
agreement and signed by eight witnesses. Certainly
there could be no plainer words, and, though Maulvi
'Abd al-Hakim withdrew from the debate on
receiving this plain assurance, yet those who had
signed the *fatwa* of *kufr* persisted in their false
charges, saying that these assurances were meant
only to deceive the public.

FURTHER WORK

Diversified work

The years that followed were years of the
greatest tribulation for Hazrat Ahmad, and, at the
same time, years of the greatest activity in his life.
He was fifty-five years of age, the age at which a

man in the Indian climate is supposed to have exhausted his energy; but, in Hazrat Ahmad's case, the time of his greatest activity begins just where it ends for others. His work became so diversified that it can hardly be supposed that he could find time for writing books. He received a large number of guests and visitors from all parts of India and he attended to them personally. He had to educate his disciples, to satisfy enquirers and to meet opponents, and he passed hours with them at meals, in regular daily walks and after the five daily prayers. As he was at the zenith of his reputation when he laid claim to Promised Messiahship, enquiries were addressed to him in very large numbers, and his mail bag, although very heavy, was disposed of by him personally till very late in life. He had to undertake journeys to meet his opponents in controversial discussions - Muslims, Christians and Arya Samajists; and, the most repugnant of all duties, he had to appear in courts to answer criminal charges and defamation suits brought against him by his opponents. Yet in the midst of all those varied occupations which would hardly seem to leave any time for serious literary work, he produced, during that period of seventeen years, over seven thousand pages, much of which was original research work, of closely printed matter in Urdu, Arabic and Persian in book form alone, while, before the age of fifty-five, he had produced only about eight hundred pages. An inexhaustible store of energy seems to have been pent up within his heart; and all this in spite of the fact that, from early youth, he was afflicted with two diseases, syncope and polyuria, which at times weakened him very much, but, when the attack was over, he was again at the helm, quite like a young man.

A few facts may be noted here showing the diversity of Hazrat Ahmad's occupations. His controversies with the orthodox 'ulama, held at Ludhiana, Delhi and Lahore, in 1891 and 1892, each lasting for several days, have already been mentioned. In 1893, he was engaged in a very important controversy with the Christian missionaries at Amritsar, and that occupied him for over two weeks. It was in that controversy that he laid down the principle that every claim as to the truth or falsehood of a religious doctrine, and the arguments for or against it, should be produced from the sacred book which a people followed, and he showed with great vigour that the Holy Qur'an alone fulfilled that condition. The proceedings of this controversy are published in a book entitled *Jang Muqaddas*, which means "Holy War".

Guru Nanak's Chola

In 1895, he turned his attention to Sikhism, another offshoot of Hinduism, which had gained considerable strength in the Punjab. His enquiries into the religious scriptures of the Sikhs led him to the conclusion that the founder of Sikhism had not only come under the influence of Muslim Sufis, but that he was in fact a Muslim, though the movement started by him took a different turn owing to political reasons. To set a seal on this conclusion, he undertook a journey to Dera Nanak, a village in the Gurdaspur District, and one of the sacred places of Sikhism. A *chola* (cloak), which is a relic of Guru Nanak himself, and which is in the custody of his descendants, is preserved there. It is a long cloak with short sleeves and is made of brown cloth. A tradition in the *Sakhi* of Bhai Bala, more commonly known as Angad's *Sakhi*, states that the *chola* was sent down to Nanak from heaven and that upon it were written the words of nature in Arabic, Turkish, Persian, Hindi and Sanskrit. Upon Nanak's death, the *chola* passed to his first successor, Angad, and thus to successive Gurus, till the time of the fifth Guru, Arjan Das. In his time, the *chola* was obtained by Tola Ram, in recognition of some great service done. After some time, it fell into the hands of Kabli Mal, a descendant of Nanak, and, since then, it has remained in the hands of his descendants at Dera Nanak. On account of the high repute and sanctity in which the *chola* was held by the followers of Nanak, the practice became common at an early date of offering coverings to protect it from wear and tear. The mystery which surrounded the *chola* became deeper by the increased number of coverings, which hid it altogether from the eye of the worshipper. Only a part of the sleeve was shown, but, by constant handling, the letters on that part became quite obscure.

As the founder of the Ahmadiyya movement had already come to the conclusion that Guru Nanak was in fact a true Muslim, he also thought of solving the mystery enshrouding the *chola*. Accordingly, on the 30th September, 1895, he started, with some of his friends, for Dera Nanak. By special arrangements made with the guardian of the *chola*, the numerous coverings, mostly of silk or fine cloth, were taken off one by one, and the actual writing on the *chola* was revealed. This was nothing but verses of the Holy Qur'an, and they were at once copied. This wonderful disclosure of the writing on the *chola* showed clearly that Nanak was a Muslim at heart. The result of the investigation was published in a book, called the *Sat Bachan*; and, though the orthodox Sikhs were greatly excited when it appeared, yet the truth of its statements concerning the *chola* has never been questioned.

Prosecutions

After this, Hazrat Ahmad had to leave Qadian on several occasions in connection with certain cases brought against him by his opponents. In 1897, he had to appear in the court of the District Magistrate of Gurdaspur to answer the charge of abetment of murder, brought forward by Dr Henry Martyn Clarke of the Church Missionary Society. The allegation was that Hazrat Mirza Ghulam Ahmad had deputed one of his disciples to murder Dr Clarke. The orthodox Muslims, represented by Maulvi Muhammad Husain of Batala, and the Arya Samajists, represented by Chaudhury Ram Bhaj Dutt, the President of the Arya Samaj, Lahore, who offered to conduct the case free of charge, joined hands with Dr Clarke. The District Magistrate, Capt. M. W. Douglas, after a thorough inquiry, found that the chief witness in the case had been schooled in his evidence by certain Christian missionaries who worked with Dr Clarke, and he acquitted Hazrat Ahmad.

In the next year, he had again to go several times to Gurdaspur and to Pathankot to answer a charge of breach of the peace, which, it was alleged by the Police, he had threatened by the publication of certain prophecies. The other party in this case was Maulvi Muhammad Husain of Batala. In January 1903, he had to appear at Jhelum to answer charges in two cases of defamation brought against him by Maulvi Karam Din. Both these cases were dismissed at the first hearing. At Jhelum, he was received with great enthusiasm by the public, and nearly one thousand persons entered into his *bai'a* in a single day. During the latter part of the year 1903, he had to appear several times at Gurdaspur in connection with another defamation case brought by the same complainant who had failed at Jhelum. On account of the academic discussions to which it gave rise, the case was protracted for nearly eighteen months. For about five months, it had a daily hearing, and, during that time, Hazrat Ahmad had to take up his residence at Gurdaspur. This case also ended in his acquittal on appeal. Thus, during the eight years, 1897 to 1904, a great part of his time was taken up by the various cases in which his opponents tried to involve him criminally, but in all of which they signally failed.

Visits to important cities

After that, he again paid visits to certain important towns to remove the misunderstandings created by false propaganda against him. He first went to Lahore, in September 1904, and there delivered a lecture to an audience of over ten thousand people of all classes and creeds. After that, in November 1904, he went to Sialkot, where he delivered the famous lecture in which he explained his mission to the Hindus, stating that the Hindu prophecies relating to the advent of a reformer were also fulfilled in his person. The underlying idea was clearly the unification of all the great nations of the world. Almost every nation expected the advent of a reformer in the latter days, and the fulfilment of the hopes of all nations in one person was certainly the best means of unifying them.

In October 1905, he went to Delhi, where, in private gatherings, he spent about two weeks in explaining his mission. On his way back from Delhi, he stopped at Ludhiana and Amritsar and delivered lectures at both places. The lecture at Amritsar had, however, to be curtailed, owing to the interference of some fanatics, and the mob outside pelted him and his companions with stones as they left the lecture-hall. His last journey was again to Lahore, in the closing days of his life, in April, 1908. For about a month, he continued at informal meetings to explain his position to the gentry of Lahore and to other visitors. The late Mian Sir Fazl-i-Husain, who was then practising as a barrister in Lahore, attended one of these meetings and asked him pointedly, whether he did or did not denounce as *kafir* all those Muslims who did not accept his claims, and he gave a categorical reply in the negative. [21] At several meetings he explained

21. About four years earlier, the same question had been put to him at Sialkot by the Mian Sahib, who was then practising there. At that time, Dr Sir Muhammad Iqbal also was present, and about two years ago, he bore testimony in a letter written to a friend that the same reply was

that he laid no claim to prophethood, and that in his writings he had used that word in only a metaphorical sense, to imply one who made a prophecy, in which sense it had previously been used by the great Muslim Sufis.

Scope of writings

In the midst of all this distraction, worry and harassment, and in spite of the persecution, which sometimes took a very serious form, he went on wielding his pen with incomparable facility and added seven thousand pages of very valuable literature to the eight hundred pages written in his earlier life which had gained him the reputation of being the greatest religious writer of his time. The value of this achievement is, however, immensely enhanced when it is realized that it deals with almost all the important religions of the world – with all the offshoots of Hinduism, such as Arya Samaj, Brahmo Samaj, Sanatan Dharm and Sikhism; with Buddhism, Judaism and Baha'ism; with all the prominent sects of Islam such as the orthodox, the Shi'as, the Kharijites, the *Ahl Hadith* and others; and last but not least with Christianity, which was his most important theme. He fought even against Atheism and Materialism.

The immense variety of the subjects dealt with is not, moreover, the only distinguishing feature of Hazrat Ahmad's religious literature. It is the originality and thoroughness with which he handles every topic that marks him out as the greatest religious writer of his time. Entirely fresh light was given then.

thrown on many Islamic subjects. Islam's outlook on religion was most liberal, and the Holy Qur'an laid down in precise words that prophets had appeared among all nations; yet the Muslims recognized the Divine origin of only the Jewish and Christian religions. It was Hazrat Mirza Ghulam Ahmad who laid stress on the point that every religion had a Divine source, though its teachings may have undergone corruption in its later history, and that, though Islam recognized the termination of prophethood in the person of the Holy Prophet Muhammad, it did not mean that God had then ceased to speak to His righteous servants, because speaking is an attribute of the Divine Being and it can never cease to function. Similarly, Hazrat Ahmad threw new light on the conception of *jihad*, which was mistakenly supposed to mean "the killing of an unbeliever who did not accept Islam". This he showed to be an entirely mistaken view. *jihad*, he showed, in the first place, conveyed the wider significance of carrying on a struggle in any field, in the broadest sense, and the struggle required for carrying to the whole world the Divine message contained in the Qur'an was the greatest of *jihads*, *jihadan kabiran*, according to the Holy Book itself. War against the unbelievers was only one phase of *jihad*, and it was allowed, he further showed, only when it was defensive. Such abstruse problems as those relating to the next life, heaven and hell, reward and punishment, resurrection, the physical, moral and spiritual conditions of man, and a number of other similar matters were discussed with a freshness and originality which drew words of praise from some of the greatest thinkers of the time. He dealt fully with all these subjects in a lecture delivered at the Conference of Religions, held in Lahore in December 1896, to which a mixed audience of all religions listened with rapt attention for two days. That lecture was translated in the *Review of Religions*, and, when that paper was sent to Count Tolstoy, he replied that he was deeply impressed by the originality of the writer. That lecture has to this day been recognized as the most powerful exposition of the teachings of Islam.

Universality of Divine revelation

In his criticism of other religions, he was equally original and forceful. Take as an example his discussion of the different offshoots of Hinduism. To Brahmoism, which denied revelation from God, he offered his own religious experience, claiming that not only did God speak to different nations of the world through their great sages and prophets in the past (which established the fact that Divine revelation was the universal experience of all nations of the world), but also that speaking was an attribute of the Divine Being and that He spoke even now as He spoke in the past, Hazrat Ahmad himself being a recipient of Divine revelation in this age. The idea of the universality of Divine revelation was, however, carried to its furthest limit when it was further explained that in its lowest form - in the form of dreams coming true and of visions - it was the universal experience of humanity.

Another modern Hindu reform movement, the Arya Samaj, arose as a revolt against Hindu idolatry and against its millions of gods, but it was Hazrat Mirza Ghulam Ahmad who pointed out that polytheism and multiplicity of gods was an idea so deep-rooted in Hinduism that even the Arya Samaj could not get rid of it, and that the doctrines of co-eternity of matter and soul with the Divine Being, and the belief that they were uncreated and self-existent like God Himself, were remnants of polytheism. On Sikhism, a three-hundred years old Hindu sect, he shed entirely new light by showing not only that its conception of Divine Unity and its other fundamental religious ideas were taken entirely from Islam, but also that its founder, Nanak, was actually a Muslim.

Death and crucifixion of Jesus

It was, however, in the sphere of his controversy with Christianity and in questions relating to the death and second advent of Christ, matters over which hung a great pall of mystery, that Hazrat Ahmad showed masterly originality and thoroughness. Muslims and Christians both believed that Jesus Christ was alive in heaven. The former held that he was taken up alive just before the crucifixion and that his semblance was thrown upon someone else who was taken for Jesus and crucified in his place. The latter believed that Jesus himself was crucified but that he was raised to life on the third day after his crucifixion and then taken up to heaven. Both further believed that he would come down to earth again before the Resurrection and destroy the Anti-Christ. The mystery surrounding Christ's death was solved by showing that, although he was nailed to the cross, he did not remain on it for a sufficiently long time to expire, that he was taken down alive and placed in a spacious room where his wounds were attended to, that by the third day he had recovered and gained sufficient strength to be present at a secret meeting of the disciples, that he then left for Afghanistan and Kashmir where the ten lost tribes of Israel had settled, and that he ultimately died a natural death, at the age of about a hundred and twenty years, in Srinagar, where his tomb is still known as the tomb of Yus Asaf. This was quite an original solution of the mystery hanging over the crucifixion and the post-crucifixion appearances of Jesus Christ. Every link in this long chain of fresh facts was established on the basis of the Holy Qur'an and Hadith, of the historical elements contained in the Gospels and of other historical, ethnological and geographical evidence, which undoubtedly required immense research work. While the mystery relating to the crucifixion of Christ was thus solved, and the central assumption that Jesus took away the sins of the world by his death on the cross, on which rested the whole structure of Church Christianity, was thus demolished at one stroke, and it was shown that the historical elements in the Gospels belied the religious doctrines attributed to them.

Advent of Messiah and Mahdi

A still deeper mystery hung over the second advent of Jesus. This subject was rendered the more complicated by its association with many others, such as those relating to the Anti-Christ, Gog and

Magog, the coming of the Mahdi, the rising of the sun from the West and so on. Hazrat Ahmad's solution of this mystery was also original. The second advent of Jesus Christ was to be taken in exactly the same sense as was the second advent of Elijah before him, which Christ himself had explained as signifying the advent of one in his spirit and power. It was a very simple explanation, yet it had never occurred to any Christian or Muslim thinker before him. The explanation of the coming of the Mahdi was also original. The Mahdi was no other than the Messiah, an idea which had never previously occurred to any Muslim in spite of the Prophet's hadith which had plainly stated that there was no Mahdi but the Messiah.

These matters having been settled, the Anti-Christ had next to be discovered. In this case, too, he was original. In the Hadith, the *Dajjal* was clearly spoken of as coming forth from a church, and this gave Hazrat Ahmad the clue to his discovery. The Church had indeed represented the teaching of Christ as just the opposite of what it actually was, and, therefore, the Church was the real Anti-Christ. The Anti-Christ being identified, there was not much difficulty in discovering the Gog and Magog. These were the two great races, the Teutons and the Slavs, who, as represented in this age by the English and the Russians, had become predominant in the world. The rising of the sun from the West meant, in symbolical language, the sun of Islam, whose shining in the West was bound up with the second advent of Christ. The West proper had remained unaffected by the message of Islam; it was through the Promised

Messiah that the Anti-Christ had to be vanquished and the way opened for the propagation of Islam in the West.

The *Review of Religions*

All these great truths were not the laborious discoveries of a great scholar which should have taken years, though a scholar Hazrat Mirza Ghulam Ahmad undoubtedly was; they blazed in upon his mind suddenly through Divine inspiration, when he was required to proclaim that Jesus Christ was dead and that he himself was the Messiah whose advent was promised in the latter days. Nor were these just the visions of a great seer. These were the grand realities, the realization of which was the great aim of Hazrat Ahmad's life. Therefore, in the midst of all those occupations and harassments to which reference has been made above, he laid with his own hands the foundations of the work of carrying the message of Islam to the West. The *Review of Religions*, a monthly magazine in English, was started in January, 1902. It was the first religious magazine in English to deal with Islamic matters, and it was conducted on rational lines which appealed equally to enlightened Muslims and to non-Muslims, and was well-suited for presenting Islam to the Western mind.

The following judgment of this paper is from the pen of a very hostile writer, H. A. Walter:

"One of the cleverest of Ahmad's followers, Maulvi Muhammad Ali, M.A., LL.B., was called to the editorship of this periodical, and at one time he was assisted by Khwaja Kamalud Din . . . This paper was well-named, for it has given its attention to a remarkably wide range of religions and to a great variety of subjects. Orthodox Hinduism, the Arya Samaj, the Brahmo Samaj and Theosophy; Sikhism, Buddhism, Jainism and Zoroastrianism; Bahaism, Christian Science and Christianity have all received attention, as well as Islam in all its ramifications, both ancient and modern, such as the Shi'ites, Ahl-i-Hadis, Kharijites, Sufis and such representative exponents of modern tendencies as Sir Syed Ahmad Khan and Syed Amir Ali."

The *Review of Religions* had thus become the mouthpiece of the Ahmadiyya movement both for removing the misconceptions that prevailed against Islam and for making a comparative study of religion. It was a preliminary step for carrying into practice the grander ideas of establishing, in the West, Muslim missions for the propagation of Islamic literature, and of translating the Holy Qur'an into European languages, ideas to which Hazrat Ahmad himself had given expression, as early as 1891, when he claimed to be the Promised Messiah, but which were carried into effect only after his death. The translation of the Holy Qur'an was taken in hand within a year after his death, while the first Muslim mission in Europe was established three years afterwards. These were the natural developments of the lines on which Hazrat Ahmad led the movement. He had nothing to do with the minor sectarian differences among the Muslims, and prepared a band of devoted followers for the spiritual conquest of the West. The seed was sown, the men were prepared who should take care of the tender plant, and the time had come for the master to depart.

FINAL DAYS

The last will

The year 1905 was coming to a close when he received certain revelations to the effect that his end was nigh. On the 24th December 1905, he published his last will, *Al-Wasiyya* (or *The Will*), in which he wrote:

"As Almighty God has informed me, in various revelations following one another, that the time of my death is near, and the revelations in that respect have been so many and so consecutive that they have shaken my being to its foundations and made this life quite indifferent to me, I have therefore thought it proper that I should write down for my friends, and for such other persons as can benefit from my teachings, some words of advice."

Below are given some of these revelations:

"The destined time of thy death has drawn nigh, and We shall not leave behind thee any mention which should be a source of disgrace to thee. Very little has remained of the time appointed for thee by thy Lord . . . And We will either let thee see a part of what We threaten them with or

We will cause thee to die . . . Very few days have remained, sorrow will overtake all on that day."

A few words of comfort are added for his disciples, and they are told that the movement will prosper after his death:

"Bear in mind, then, my friends, that it being an established Divine law that He shows two manifestations of His power so that He may thus bring to naught two false pleasures of the opponents, it is not possible that He should neglect this old law now. Be not, therefore, grieved at what I have said, and let not your hearts feel sorrow, for it is necessary for you to see a second manifestation of Divine power, and it is better for you, for it is perpetual and will not be intercepted to the day of judgment."

The arrangements for the carrying on of the movement are then suggested. The first point was initiation into the movement. While the founder was alive, he personally initiated new members into the movement. After his death, he directed that members should be initiated by the righteous from among his followers. And he wrote:

"Such men will be elected by the agreement of the faithful. Anyone, therefore, about whom forty of the faithful should agree that he is fit to accept bai'a from other people in my name shall be entitled to do so, and he ought to make himself a model for others."

Anjuman to carry on work after him

The second point was the management of the affairs connected with the movement, and for this an Anjuman was established with full powers to deal with all such topics. This Anjuman was formed under the name of *Sadr Anjuman Ahmadiyya* (or, *The Chief Society of the Ahmadis*), and the rules and regulations controlling it were given under Hazrat Ahmad's own signature. It began to function immediately after the publication of *The Will*, exercising full authority over all the affairs of the movement, including its finances. When a dispute arose, about twenty months after the Anjuman was formed, as to the extent of its powers, and the matter was referred to the founder, he gave his decision in the following words:

"My opinion is that any matter about which the Anjuman comes to a decision that it should be thus, such decision having been taken by a majority of votes, the same should be considered as the right decision, and the same should be the final decision. Nevertheless, I would add this much that, in certain religious matters which are related to the special object of my advent, I should be informed. I am fully confident that this Anjuman will not do anything against my wishes. This is written only by way of precaution, for it may be that the matter is one which is ordained by God in a special manner. This rule is to be observed only during my lifetime; after that, the decision of this Anjuman in all matters shall be final."

The Anjuman was thus entrusted with the fullest powers in all affairs relating to the movement, and in his own words "the Anjuman was the successor of the Divinely-appointed Khalifa".

Message of peace

As already noted, in April 1908, he went to Lahore. There, while occupied from day to day in explaining his position to eager Muslim listeners, who wondered when they heard from his own lips that he was not a claimant to prophethood, he began writing a pamphlet, containing a special message for his Hindu countrymen, aiming at bringing about lasting union between the Hindus and the Muslims. The message was based on the broad Qur'anic principle which he had been preaching all his life that all religions emanated from a Divine source, as the Holy Qur'an clearly said: "And there is not a nation but a warner has gone among them" (35:24). In accordance with this verse, he held that prophets must have appeared in India, and, as Rama and Krishna were the two great reformers recognized by the Hindus, they must have been the prophets sent to that people. He called upon the Hindus to reciprocate the Muslim recognition of the Hindu prophets by recognizing the prophethood of the Holy Prophet Muhammad. If they did that, a lasting peace could be achieved between the Hindus and the Muslims, in which case he and his followers were prepared to make a further concession to Hindu religious sentiment by giving up their lawful right of slaughtering cows and using beef as an article of food. This message was aptly named the

"Message of Peace", and it proved to be his last message.

Founder's demise

At the age of seventy-three, he was still wielding his pen in the cause of Islam with the energy of a man of thirty. He had just finished the last lines of his *Message of Peace*, outlining the possible basis of an everlasting peace between the Hindus and the Muslims, when suddenly he fell ill at 10 p.m. on the evening of the 25th May, with an attack of diarrhoea, to which he succumbed at 10 a.m. on the morning of 26th May, 1908. The Civil Surgeon of Lahore certified that death was not due to an infectious disease, and it was on the production of this certificate that the authorities permitted the carrying of his body to Qadian, where it was consigned to its last resting-place, on the 27th May.

CONTRIBUTION TO ISLAM

Mysteries unravelled

Thus ended an eventful life which in the short space of eighteen years - 1890 to 1908 - not only had revolutionized many of the existing religious ideas but had even taken definite steps in an entirely new direction - the presenting of Islam to, and the spiritual conquest of, the West. Deep religious mysteries which had baffled human minds for centuries had been unravelled. The second advent of Christ, the tribulation of the Anti-Christ, the prevalence of Gog and Magog, the coming of the Mahdi and similar other topics were mysteries which affected the two great religions of the world, Christianity and Islam, both contending for the mastery of the world, and an inspired man was indeed needed to lift the veil from the face of these mysteries. Such a man was Hazrat Mirza Ghulam Ahmad. He was gifted not only with inspiration to elucidate the deepest mysteries, but also with the faith and energy which enabled him to give a new direction to the dissemination of Islam, which had hitherto found the West deaf to its message. Christianity was out to conquer the Muslim world; in temporal matters it had ousted Islam, but in the spiritual domain, Hazrat Mirza Ghulam Ahmad made a bold start and gave a challenge to Christianity in its very home. It is as a result of that challenge that mosques are being built in the great centres of Christianity, that a vital change is being brought about in the attitude of Europe towards Islam, and that thousands of cultured and advanced Europeans are finding a haven of peace under its banner.

NOT A PROPHET

His claim misunderstood

Every great man has been misunderstood to a certain extent, and so has Hazrat Ahmad. The most serious of these misunderstandings is that which states that he claimed to be a prophet. This charge was laid against him by his opponents when he first claimed to be the Promised Messiah, and a section of his followers, the Qadianis, have now joined hands with them in bringing discredit upon his movement. We have already noted, while discussing his claims, that he claimed to be a *mujaddid* in 1882, and that his claim to Promised Messiahship was advanced in 1891. It was on the occasion of the latter claim that he was charged by his opponents with laying claim to prophethood, and he forthwith denounced that as a false charge, declaring definitely and unmistakenly that he had never claimed to be a prophet, that he believed in the Holy Prophet Muhammad as the final Prophet, and that he looked upon any claimant to prophethood after him as a liar. A few quotations from his writings have already been given. After reading those statements, no one can honestly attribute to him a claim to prophethood.

How then did the misunderstanding arise? When Hazrat Ahmad laid claim to Promised Messiahship on the ground of his being the like of Jesus Christ, an objection was brought forward that Jesus Christ was a prophet and that none but a prophet could be his like. The following answer to this objection is met with in the first book in which a claim to Promised Messiahship is advanced:

"Here, if it be objected that the like of Christ must also be a prophet because Christ was a prophet, the reply to this in the first place is that our Lord and Master has not laid it down that the coming Messiah shall be a prophet; nay, he has made it clear that he shall be a Muslim and shall be bound by the law of Islam like ordinary Muslims . . . Besides this, there is no doubt that I have come as a *muhaddath* from God, and *muhaddath* is, in one sense, a prophet, though he does not possess perfect prophethood; but still he is partially a prophet, for he is endowed with the gift of being spoken to by God, matters relating to the unseen are revealed to him, and, like the revelation of prophets and apostles, his revelation is kept free from the interference of the devil, and the kernel of the law is disclosed to him, and he is commissioned just like the prophets, and like prophets it is incumbent on him that he should announce his claim at the top of his voice." [22]

Denial of prophethood

It should be borne in mind that in the terminology of the Islamic law a *muhaddath* is a righteous person who is not a prophet but who is spoken to by God. When confronted with the objection that he claimed to be the like of Christ but that Christ was a prophet, and therefore his like must also be a prophet, Hazrat Ahmad offered the above explanation, the gist of which is that he was a *muhaddath* and that the *muhaddath* was, in one sense, a prophet, though his prophethood was partial and not perfect. It was this statement which was misinterpreted by his opponents as a claim to prophethood, and, on this basis, he was denounced as a *kafir* or heretic. To remove the misunderstanding, he emphatically denied again and again that he was a claimant to prophethood and

22. *Tauzih Maram,* pp. 9-10.

emphasized that he claimed to be only a *muhaddath*:

"I make a public declaration in this house of God, the mosque, that I believe in the finality of prophethood of the Last of the Prophets (may peace and the blessings of God be upon him), and that I consider the person who denies the finality of prophethood to be a faithless man and one outside the pale of Islam." [23]

"I have laid no claim to prophethood; my claim is to be a *muhaddath*, and this I have made by Divine command. There is no doubt that *muhaddathiyya* also contains a strong part of prophethood . . .
"If, then, this be called prophethood metaphorically, or be regarded as a strong part of prophethood, does it amount to a claim to prophethood?" [24]

"Be it known to all Muslims that all such words as occur in my writings . . . to this effect, that the *muhaddath* is, in one sense, a prophet, or that *muhaddathiyya* is partial prophethood or imperfect prophethood, all these words are not to be taken in their proper (technical) sense, but they have been used merely in their literal significance . . . Therefore, I have not the least hesitation in stating my meaning in another form for the conciliation of my Muslim brethren, and that other form is that, wherever the word *nabi* (prophet) is used in my writings, it should be

23. Manifesto, copied in *Din al-Haq*, p. 29.
24. *Izala Auham*, pp. 421-422.

taken as meaning *muhaddath*, and the word *nabi*
(prophet) should be regarded as having been
blotted out." [25]

"One of the objections of those who call me a
kafir is that I lay claim to prophethood and say
that I am a prophet. The reply to this is that it
should be known that I have not laid claim to
prophethood, nor have I said that I am a prophet,
but these people have made haste to make a
mistake in understanding my words ... I have
said naught to these people except what I have
written in my books, that I am a *muhaddath* and
that God speaks to me as He speaks to a
muhaddath . . . and what right have I that I
should lay claim to prophethood and get out of
the pale of Islam?" [26]

"These people have not understood my words and
they say that I am a claimant to prophethood,
and this allegation of theirs is a clear lie." [27]

These are only a few of the numerous statements
made by Hazrat Ahmad clearly denying any claim to
prophethood. It is further explained in these
statements that, when he called the *muhaddath* "in
one sense a prophet", he was using the word
"prophet" in a literal sense, not in its proper or
technical sense, and this is also called a
metaphorical use of the word. It was the height of
folly on the part of his opponents, and no less is it

25. Manifesto, dated 3rd February, 1892.
26. *Hamamat al-Bushra*, p. 81.
27. *Ibid.*

on the part of his followers belonging to the Qadian section, to take the word in a real sense when the person who uses it expressly states it to have been used in a metaphorical sense. This position he maintained to the last. Thus, in one of his last writings, the *Haqiqat al-Wahy*, published less than a year before his death, he wrote:

> "This servant does not say aught but what the Holy Prophet said, and he does not go a single step out of his guidance; and he says that God has called him a prophet by His revelation, and I have been called so by the tongue of our Messenger, Mustafa; and he means naught by prophethood but that he is frequently spoken to by God . . . and we do not mean by prophethood what is meant by it in the former Scriptures."[28]

> "And God does not mean by my prophethood anything but being frequently spoken to by Him, and the curse of God is on him who intends aught more than this . . . and our Messenger is the last of the prophets and the chain of messengers has come to an end in him . . . and nothing remains after him but being frequently spoken to by God, and that, too, on condition of being a follower of his . . . and I have been called a prophet of God in a metaphorical sense, not in the real sense."[29]

These few quotations should set all doubts at rest with regard to Hazrat Ahmad's alleged claim to prophethood. He claimed to be only a *muhaddath*,

28. *Haqiqat al-Wahy*, Supplement, p. 16.
29. *Ibid.*, pp. 64-65.

but, as the word *nabi* (prophet) occurred in some of
his revelations, as also in a hadith of the Holy
Prophet in relation to the coming Messiah, he
explained that it was used metaphorically, not in
the real sense of the word, and that metaphorically
a *muhaddath* could be called a prophet because he
was spoken to by God. Therefore, wherever he used
the word "prophet" regarding himself, it was in a
metaphorical sense. Never did he mean by it that he
was a prophet in the real sense of the word, but
only that he was spoken to by God; and that God
speaks to His servants in this *umma* is a fact
generally admitted by all Muslims.

JIHAD

Doctrine of Jihad not abrogated

   Another charge against the founder of the
Ahmadiyya movement is that he denied the doctrine
of *jihad*. It is easy to see that anyone who accepts
the Holy Qur'an and the Holy Prophet Muhammad
cannot deny *jihad*, injunctions relating to which
occupy a considerable portion of the Holy Qur'an.
The orthodox Muslims believe that some verses of
the Holy Qur'an have been abrogated by others. The
Ahmadiyya movement has long been fighting against
this doctrine, and many enlightened Muslims now
accept the Ahmadi view that no verse, not even one
word or one jot of the Holy Qur'an was abrogated.
Under the heading, "A statement of some of our
beliefs", the founder of the Ahmadiyya movement
wrote:

"God speaks to His servants in this *umma*, and they are given the semblance of prophets, and they are not really prophets, for the Qur'an has made perfect the needs of Law, and they are given only an understanding of the Qur'an, and they cannot add to, or detract from it aught; and whoever adds to, or detracts from it, he is of the devils who are wicked."[30]

It is therefore impossible that, holding such a belief, Hazrat Mirza Ghulam Ahmad could say that he abrogated *jihad*, which was made obligatory by the Holy Qur'an and which was one of the five fundamentals of Islam. I quote a passage from his pamphlet entitled *The Jihad* to show that he differed from the *'ulama* only in his interpretation of *jihad* as inculcated by the Holy Qur'an:

"It should be remembered that the doctrine of *jihad* as understood by the Muslim *'ulama* of our day, who call themselves Maulvis, is not true . . . These people are so persistent in their belief, which is entirely wrong and against the Qur'an and Hadith, that the man who does not believe in it and is against it is called a *Dajjal.*"[31]

Misconceptions about Jihad

It would appear from this that, according to the founder of the Ahmadiyya movement, the doctrine of *jihad* as understood by the *'ulama* was opposed to the true teachings of the Holy Qur'an and Hadith.

30. *Mawahib al-Rahman*, pp. 66-67.

31. *The Jihad*, pp. 5-6.

What Hazrat Ahmad rejected was not the doctrine of *jihad* but the orthodox interpretation thereof, which had given rise in the West to grave misconceptions regarding the doctrine of *jihad*, so that even unprejudiced Western writers thought the word *jihad* to be synonymous with war undertaken for forcing the religion of Islam upon non-Muslims. Thus, in the *Encyclopaedia of Islam*, the article on "Jihad" opens with the following words: "The spread of Islam by arms is a religious duty upon Muslims in general". Klein, in his *Religion of Islam*, makes an even more sweeping statement: "Jihad ... The fighting against unbelievers with the object of either winning them over to Islam, or subduing and exterminating them in case they refuse to become Muslims."

In the Muslim popular mind there was an even greater misconception, that the killing of an unbeliever was *jihad* and that such an act entitled the perpetrator to be called a *ghazi*. This conception, coupled with the prevailing belief in the advent of a Mahdi who would put all non-Muslims to the sword if they refused to accept Islam, opposed as it was to the plain teachings of the Holy Qur'an, was doing immense harm to the cause of the spread of Islam among non-Muslims. With very few exceptions, even educated Muslims were victims of the wrong impression that Islam enjoined aggressive war against non-believers, and the founder of the Ahmadiyya movement had to carry on incessant war, not against *jihad* as inculcated by the Holy Qur'an, but against the false conceptions of it prevalent among both Muslims and non-Muslims.

War to spread religion never allowed

The way was cleared for removing these misconceptions by establishing two principles: *(1)* That *jihad* means *exerting oneself to the extent of one's ability and power, whether it is by word or deed*, and that the word is used in this broad sense in the Holy Qur'an; *(2)* that when it is used in the narrower sense of *fighting*, it means fighting only in self-defence. If, therefore, all exertions to carry the message of Islam to non-Muslims by simple preaching, or what may be called spiritual warfare, fell within the purview of *jihad*, a war carried on for the propagation of Islam, if such a one was ever undertaken by a Muslim ruler, was quite outside the scope of its true significance, as it was against the basic principle laid down in the Holy Qur'an that "there is no compulsion in religion" (2:256). If Hazrat Ahmad ever spoke of the abrogation of *jihad*, it was of this misconception of the word *jihad*, not of the *jihad* as inculcated by the Holy Qur'an, every word of which he believed to be a Divine revelation which could not be abrogated till the day of judgment. Here is another passage from the pamphlet quoted above:

"Their contention that, since *jihad* was permitted in the early days [of Islam], there is no reason why it should be prohibited now is entirely misconceived. It may be refuted in two ways; firstly, that this inference is drawn from wrong premises and our Holy Prophet never used the sword against any people, except those who first took up the sword [against the Muslims] ...

secondly, that, even if we suppose for the sake of argument that there was such a *jihad* in Islam as these Maulvis think, even so that order does not stand now, for it is written that, when the Promised Messiah appears, there will be an end of *jihad* with the sword and of religious wars." [32]

It will be seen that the prevalent idea that Islam allowed a *jihad* for the spread of religion is refuted in two ways. In the first place, it is stated that this conception of *jihad* is against the Holy Qur'an and Hadith, as the Holy Prophet raised the sword only in self-defence, not for the propagation of religion. Further, it is added that, even if for the sake of argument it is supposed that a *jihad* for the propagation of religion was ever undertaken – that such was never undertaken by the Holy Prophet has been definitely stated in the first part – such *jihad* cannot be undertaken now, for it is said of the Promised Messiah that he will put down (religious) wars, *yaz' al-harb*, as plainly stated in the *Bukhari*. What is aimed at is really this, that a *jihad* contrary to the teachings of the Holy Qur'an and to the practice of the Holy Prophet, if ever there was one, was undoubtedly the result of some misconception, and, according to the hadith quoted above, the Promised Messiah will remove that misconception and thus put an end to such wars.

Conditions of Jihad

This position is made still more clear in an Arabic letter, addressed to the Muslims of the world, and

32. *The Jihad*, p. 6.

forming a supplement to his book, *Tuhfa Golarwiyya*. In this letter he says:

"There is not the least doubt that the conditions laid down for *jihad* [in the Holy Qur'an] are not to be met with at the present time and in this country; so it is illegal for the Muslims to fight for [the propagation of] religion and to kill anyone who rejects the Sacred Law, for God has made clear the illegality of *jihad* when there is peace and security."[33]

It is here made clear that *jihad* with the sword is allowed by Islam only under certain conditions, and, as those conditions are not met with at the present time in the country in which the writer lives, therefore *jihad* with the sword is illegal here at the present time. This argument leads to the definite conclusion that *jihad* may be legal in another country in which exist the necessary conditions laid down in the Holy Qur'an, or even here when the conditions have changed. These conditions are expressly stated in the Holy Book: "And fight in the way of God against those who fight against you, and be not aggressive, for God does not love the aggressors" (2:191).

Muslims expressed loyalty to British rule

In this connection may be mentioned another charge relative to his attitude towards the British Government in India. As stated at the beginning of this book, the Sikhs, who ruled the Punjab before

33. *Tuhfa Golarwiyya*, Supplement, p. 30.

the advent of the British rule, had not only ousted
Hazrat Ahmad's family from their estate, but, in
their later days, there was such lawlessness in the
country as made life impossible for the Muslims,
who were not allowed the free exercise of their
religion, and whose very culture was on the verge
of being swept away. It was at such a time that the
British Government stepped in and saved the
Muslims from annihilation. Thus, people who with
their own eyes had seen the woes of the Muslims, or
even their desendants, considered the British
Government as a blessing, for through it they were
saved. For allowing full liberty of religion and
conscience and for establishing peace where before
there were anarchy and lawlessness, Hazrat Mirza
Ghulam Ahmad was not alone in praising the English
rule. All writers of that time considered it their
duty to give vent to similar expressions of loyalty
and thankfulness. Sir Syed Ahmad Khan, who
occupied a position among the Muslims which has
not been vouchsafed to any other leader since his
time, wrote exactly in the same strain as did Hazrat
Mirza Ghulam Ahmad. Even the Wahabis, who
remained for a long time in the bad books of the
Government, declared from the housetops their
loyalty to the Government. Thus wrote Maulvi
Muhammad Jabbar, the famous Wahabi leader:

"Before all, I thank the Government under which
we can publicly and with the beat of drums teach
the religious doctrines of our pure faith without
any interference whatsoever, and we can pay
back our opponents whether they are Christians
or others in their own coin. Such religious liberty

we cannot have even under the Sultan of Turkey."[34]

Another famous *Ahl Hadith* leader, Maulvi Muhammad Husain of Batala, wrote:

"Considering the Divine Law and the present condition of the Muslims, we have said that this is not the time of the sword."[35]

Nawab Siddiq Hasan Khan, another great leader and writer, went even further:

"A perusal of the historical books shows that the peace, security and liberty which all people have received under this rule have never been obtained under any other rule."[36]

"Whoever goes against it [i.e., loyalty and faithfulness to the British rule], not only is a mischief-maker in the eyes of the rulers, but he shall also be farthest from what Islam requires and from the way of the faithful, and he shall be regarded as a violator of the covenant, unfaithful in his religion and a perpetrator of the greatest sin, and what his condition will be on the day of judgment will become evident there."[37]

There was another reason why Hazrat Mirza Ghulam Ahmad had to lay special stress on loyalty to the British rule. He claimed to be the Promised

34. *Barakat-i-Islam*, Title page, 2.
35. *Isha'at al-Sunna*, Safar, 1301 A.H., p. 366.
36. *Tarjuman Wahabia*, p. 8.   37. *Op. cit.*, pp. 23-24.

Mahdi, and, as the name of Mahdi was associated with the sword, the Government for many years regarded the Ahmadiyya movement with distrust, thinking that the founder might at any time rise in revolt against it. It was to remove this wrong impression that Hazrat Ahmad laid much stress on his faithfulness to the British rule. Moreover, he was laying the foundations of a missionary society with the grand aim of spreading Islam throughout the world, and such a society could do its work only by remaining loyal to the Government established by law in any country and by remaining aloof from all political agitation.

CHRISTIAN ASSAULT ON ISLAM

Vituperative Christian propaganda

Another charge against the founder of the Ahmadiyya movement is that he makes slanderous attacks on the blessed person of Christ. This again is a gross misrepresentation of what he wrote. How can a man who professes the faith of Islam abuse a prophet of God, when he is required to believe in that prophet? Jesus Christ is expressly mentioned in the Holy Qur'an as a prophet, and every Muslim must honour him as such. In order to understand the nature of the two writings to which objection is taken, two points must be clearly borne in mind. The first is the nature of the controversy which was carried on by the Christian missionaries in India, in the last quarter of the nineteenth century. The preaching of the Christian missionary until a short time ago was of a quite different character from

what it is today. In those days, the Christian
missionary was under the impression that the darker
the picture he drew of the Prophet of Islam, the
greater would be his success in winning over
converts from among the Muslims; and this
impression became stronger as the missionary
reviewed the results. Not only some well-to-do
people from among the Muslims, but even some
Maulvis of great repute went over to the Christian
camp, and, to win the favour of their European
masters, these new disciples carried the
vituperative propaganda against Islam to an
extreme which made the Muslim blood boil. Some of
the Christian controversial books of those days must
indeed be ranked as the filthiest literature that has
ever been produced, apart from the fact that the
founder of the Arya Samaj and some of his blind
votaries imitated the Christian missionary, and,
later on, the Arya Samajist preacher even surpassed
the Christian missionary in the art of vituperation.

It is difficult even to conceive today how all
those things could be written in the name of
religion. The *Masih al-Dajjal* by Ramchand (1873),
Sirat al-Masih wal Muhammad by Rev. Thakurdas
(1882), *Andruna Bible* by Abdullah Atham, in which
an attempt has been made to show that our Holy
Prophet was the Anti-Christ and the Dragon of the
Revelation, *Muhammad Ki Tawarih Ka Ijmal* by Rev.
William (1891), *Taftish al-Islam* by Rev. Rodgers
(1870), *Nabiyy Ma'thum*, published by the American
Mission Press of Ludhiana (1884), and dozens of
other books and hundreds of tracts, are all strings
of abusive epithets heaped upon the Holy Prophet
and his companions, each writer trying to outdo the

others in scurrility. To call the Holy Prophet an impostor, *Dajjal* or Anti-Christ, a deceiver, a dacoit, the slave of his sensual passions whose lust knew no bounds, and to attribute every conceivable crime to him became a habit with these Christian controversialists. Page after page of the writings named above and of others of the same type are full of such descriptions as the following:

"If he [the Prophet of Islam] abrogated the Gospels there is no wonder, for all those who are bent low on the world and are worshippers of lust do like this."

"Sensual lust . . . is to be met with in Muhammad to an excessive degree so that he was always its slave. Muhammad, like other Arabs, from his very appearance seems to be a lover of women."

"The occasion of the law relating to marriage with an adopted son's wife was the flaming of the lust of Muhammad on seeing Zainab naked."

"The religion of the Pope and the religion of Muhammad are two jaws of the Dragon."

"Ring-leader of dacoits, a robber, a killer of people by secret conspiracies."

"When by chance his eye caught a glance of her beauty, sinful love took possession of his heart, and to have his wicked desire fulfilled he arranged to get permission from Heaven."

"We cannot give any name to his claim to prophethood except fraud or cunning."

"All this is the fabrication of Muhammad; he was a slave of his passions."

"His character in no way befits the office of a prophet; he was a slave of his passions, full of the spirit of revenge and a selfish man, an extreme follower of his low desires. The Qur'an is a falsehood, his own fabrication, which encouraged his slavery to passion and his lust."

"His speech and his ways increased in wickedness with his age."

This is only a sample of the writings of the Christian missionaries of those days. In fact, so scurrilous was this literature growing that, when Rev. Imad-ud-Din, a Maulvi who had become a convert to Christianity, published his writings, they were found to be so grossly abusive that even Christians began to complain of them, and the *Shams al-Akbar* of Lucknow, itself a Christian missionary paper, was compelled to give a warning against the offensiveness of Imad-ud-Din's writings, saying that "if there was again a mutiny like that of 1857, it would be due to the abusive and scurrilous language of his writings".

Muslims' love for the Prophet

There was not the least exaggeration in the warning given by this Christian paper. The Muslim is never so offended as when his Prophet is abused. He can submit to the greatest insult, but the one thing to which he will not submit is the abuse of the Holy Prophet Muhammad. Recent years have brought before us many instances of this deep-rooted love of the Muslim for his Prophet. How many young Muslims have lost their mental balance and turned a revolver against the reviler of the Prophet, knowing fully well that they must pay for this with their lives? Nobody can gauge the depth of the love of a Muslim for his Prophet. It is a fact that the sting of the Prophet's abuse affects the Muslim's heart so deeply that he gets excited beyond all measure, and cognizance of this fact should be taken by the highest executive authority, even if the High Courts of Justice cannot give a more liberal interpretation to the law of the land and must inflict a death penalty on youths who have become mentally unbalanced by such excitement.

Criticism directed at the "imaginary Messiah"

It would have been no wonder if the highly scurrilous tenour of Christian controversialists had excited a Muslim defender of the Faith like the founder of the Ahmadiyya movement to such an extent that he made remarks unworthy of himself and of the cause which he supported. Nevertheless, he kept his mental balance and adopted a method of controversy which, within a very short time, made the Christian missionaries realize that their methods needed changing, and this is the second point which must be borne in mind. It was a simple method. What would be the picture of Jesus Christ if he were criticised and found fault with in the manner in which the Christian missionaries criticized and found fault with the Holy Prophet of Islam? In fact, nothing short of this could make the Christian missionary realize how deeply he was offending the Muslim feeling. Therefore, when Hazrat Ahmad first adopted this method, he wrote in plain words:

"As the Rev. Fateh Masih of Fatehgarh in the Gurdaspur district has written to us a very scurrilous letter, and in it he has accused our Lord and Master, the Holy Prophet Muhammad, of adultery, and has used about him many other scurrilous words by way of abuse, it is, therefore, advisable that a reply to his letter should be published. This pamphlet has therefore been written. I hope that Christian missionaries will read it carefully and will not be offended by its words, for this method is entirely the result of the harsh words and filthy abuse of Fateh Masih. Still, we have every regard for the sacred glory of Jesus Christ, and in return for the abusive words of Fateh Masih, only an imaginary Messiah (*farzi Masih*) has been spoken of."[38]

This position was again and again made clear by Hazrat Ahmad in his writings, but interested persons carry on false propaganda, ignoring the explanation. Thus M. Zafar 'Ali of *Zamindar* attributes the following words to Hazrat Ahmad:

"Jesus Christ was evil-minded and overbearing.

38. *Nur al-Qur'an*, p. 1.

He was the enemy of the righteous. We cannot
call him even a gentleman, much less a prophet
(*Anjam Atham*, p. 9)."

Anyone who refers to page 9 of the book referred
to will find that the writer is guilty of making a
false allegation. The passage as met with in the
book runs thus:

"In the same way, the impious Fateh Masih has,
in his letter to me, called our Holy Prophet
adulterer and has abused him in many other ways.
Thus this filthy section . . . compel us to write
something about their Yasu' [Jesus], and let the
Muslims know that God has not made any mention
of this Yasu' in the Holy Qur'an. The Christian
missionaries say that Yasu' was that person who
claimed to be God and called Holy Moses a thief
and a cheat, and disbelieved in the advent of the
Holy Prophet, and said that after him only false
prophets would come. We cannot call such an
evil-minded, overbearing person, and the enemy
of the righteous, a gentleman - still less a
prophet."

Between the quotation given by M. Zafar 'Ali and
the passage actually found in the book, there is the
difference between heaven and earth. The founder
of the Ahmadiyya movement never wrote that Jesus
Christ was evil-minded and overbearing. On the
other hand, adhering to the principle which he had
made clear in the *Nur al-Qur'an*, as quoted above,
he merely tells his opponent, Fateh Masih, that the
imaginary Messiah of the Christians (*farzi Masih*),

who is not the same as the Messiah of the Holy
Qur'an (the real Messiah), may, on the basis of the
Christian writings, be described as an evil-minded
and overbearing person, if the method of criticism
adopted by the Christians in the case of the Holy
Prophet Muḥammad, whom they called an adulterer,
was to be followed in the case of their Christ. It is
the imaginary Messiah which the Christian
missionary has drawn that is condemned by the
founder of the Ahmadiyya movement, and not the
Messiah himself. Now, according to the Muslim
faith, if a man calls himself God and also denounces
the righteous servants of God as being thieves and
cheats, he is undoubtedly an overbearing and evil-
minded man. The Muslims believe, and so did the
founder of the Ahmadiyya movement, that Jesus
Christ never said he was God, and he never
denounced the other righteous servants of God;
therefore they hold that the picture of the Messiah
drawn by the Christians is not the picture of a man
who actually lived, but of one who exists only in
the Christian imagination. It is this imaginary
picture which Hazrat Ahmad denounces, and that,
too, he did merely because the Christian
missionaries would not refrain from abusing the
Holy Prophet of Islam.

It should be borne in mind that this method of
paying back the Christian missionaries in their own
coin was adopted by other recognized Muslim
leaders before the founder of the Ahmadiyya
movement. Thus, Maulana Rahmat Allah writes in
the introduction to his book, *Izala Auham*:

"As the Christian missionaries are disrespectful

in their speeches and writings towards the best of men, our Holy Prophet, and towards the Holy Qur'an and Hadith of the Prophet ... so we have been compelled to pay them back in the same coin ... By no means is it my belief that I should speak of a prophet in disparaging terms."

Very recently, even the official organ of the *Jami'at al-'Ulama* of Delhi, *al-Jam'iyya*, dated 20th Nov. 1932, wrote in reply to certain Christian missionaries:

"The person whom the Christians erroneously take for the Messiah was really the enemy of the Messiah and he has nothing to do with Islam and the Qur'an. Nor does any Muslim believe in him."

DISSERVICE OF 'ULAMA

Zafar 'Ali's false propaganda

An example of how false propaganda is being carried on against the founder of the Ahmadiyya movement is the statement published very widely by M. Zafar 'Ali in his paper, the *Zamindar*, bearing the heading, "An open letter to the King of England", in which he states that Hazrat Mirza Ghulam Ahmad accused Mary of adultery and called Christ a bastard. When he was challenged to produce a single quotation in support of this statement, he remained silent, though he continued to repeat the false allegation. It is clear on the face of it that a Muslim who believed in the Holy Qur'an could not make such a wild statement as that attributed to the founder of the Ahmadiyya movement, but the public is being fed on these lies by the sworn enemies of the movement. Far from accusing Mary of adultery and calling Jesus a bastard, Hazrat Mirza Ghulam Ahmad again and again speaks of the miraculous birth of Jesus Christ. The following three quotations will suffice for this purpose:

"One of the doctrines we hold is that Jesus Christ and John the Baptist were both born miraculously ... And the secret in creating Jesus and John in this manner was the manifestation of a great sign ... And the first thing He [God] did to bring this about was the creation of Jesus without a father through the manifestation of Divine power only." [39]

The ground on which this is based is his [Jesus Christ's] creation without the agency of a human father, and the detail of this is that a certain section of the Jews, i.e., the Sadducees, were deniers of the Resurrection, so God informed them through some of His prophets that a son from among their community would be born without a father, and this would be a sign of the truth of Resurrection." [40]

"The [Arya Samajist] lecturer also objected to Mary bearing a child by the Holy Spirit and to Jesus being born from Mary alone. The reply is that this was done by the same God who,

39. *Mawahib al-Rahman*, pp. 70-72.
40. *Hamamat al-Bushra*, p. 90.

according to the Arya Samaj teachings, creates millions of people in the beginning of every new creation, just as vegetables grow out of the earth. If, according to the Vedic teachings, God has created the world millions of times, nay times without number, in this manner, and there was no need that men and women should unite together in order that a child should be born, where is the harm if Jesus Christ was born similarly?"[41]

The above quotations should be sufficient to convince even the greatest enemy of the movement that its founder sincerely believed that Jesus Christ was born of Mary without her coming into union with a male. Hazrat Ahmad not only states his own belief on this matter, but he replies to the objections of the Arya Samaj, and lays stress on the point that Jesus Christ was born without a human father. How could he then accuse Mary of adultery when he states again and again that she had not even a lawful union with a man before the birth of Jesus Christ? In the face of these clear statements, to say that he regarded Mary as having committed adultery or that he called Jesus Christ a bastard is a bare-faced lie, yet it is stuff such as this that the public is expected to take, and actually takes, for Gospel truth.

'Ulama abuse the Promised Messiah

Another charge against Hazrat Ahmad is that, in his dealings with the orthodox 'ulama, he was very severe. As a matter of fact, the founder of the

41. *Chashma Ma'rifa*, p. 217.

Ahmadiyya movement, in this case also, paid back the opposing *'ulama* in their own coin. No sooner had he announced that Jesus Christ was dead and that he himself was the Messiah who was to appear among the Muslims than they denounced him in the most scurrilous terms and applied to him every hateful epithet which they could think of. The following are only a few examples taken from the pages of *Isha'at al-Sunna*, a periodical issued by Maulvi Muhammad Husain of Batala, which had become the mouthpiece of the *'ulama*:

"Hidden enemy of Islam"; "The second Musailima"; "*Dajjal*"; "a liar"; "a cheat"; "accursed one"; "he should have his face blackened, and a rope should be tied round his neck and a necklace of shoes put over him, and in this condition he should be carried through the towns of India"; "a satan, an evil-doer"; "Zindeeq"; "most shameless"; "worse than *Dajjal*"; "has the manners of ruffians and scavengers, nay those of beasts and savages"; "progeny of Halaku Khan and Changez Khan, the unbelieving Turks, this shows that you are really a . . ."

The literature produced against Hazrat Ahmad teemed with such scurrilous epithets, and even worse than these; no abusive word could be thought of which was not applied to him merely because he claimed to be the Promised Messiah. In addition to this, *fatwas* were issued against the founder and the members of the Ahmadiyya movement, declaring them to be too polluted to set foot in a mosque, declaring even their dead bodies to be unfit for a Muslim graveyard, and pronouncing their marriages to be illegal and their property to be lawful spoil for others, so that it was no sin to take it away by any means.

'Ulama as described in Hadith

It was 'ulama of this type whom the founder of the Ahmadiyya movement sometimes dealt with severely, and, if he occasionally made a retort in kind and gave a bad name to such irresponsible people who had lost all sense of decency, he could not be blamed according to any moral code. Thus he writes in one of his latest books:

"Those 'ulama of the latter days whom the Holy Prophet has called the *Yahud* [Jews] of this *umma* are particularly those Maulvis who are opponents of the Promised Messiah and are his sworn enemies and who are doing everything possible to bring him to naught and call him *kafir*, unbeliever and *Dajjal* . . . But those 'ulama who do not belong to this category, we cannot call them the *Yahud* of this *umma*". [42]

Elsewhere, explaining his attitude, he says:

"This our description of them does not apply to the righteous but to the mischievous among them." [43]

42. *Barahin Ahmadiyya*, Part 5, p. 114.
43. *Al-Huda*, p. 68.

It cannot be denied that a certain class of 'ulama is spoken of in very strong words in Hadith itself. Thus, in one hadith, the 'ulama of the latter days are described as "the worst of all under the canopy of heaven", and it is added: "From among them would the tribulation come forth and into them would it turn back." [44] According to another hadith, the Holy Prophet is reported to have said: "There will come upon my umma a time of great trial, and the people will have recourse to their 'ulama, and lo! they will find them to be apes and swine." [45]

'Ulama's disservice to Islam

There is almost a consensus of opinion that what was stated about the evil condition of 'ulama had come true in the present age. Writing shortly prior to the founder of the Ahmadiyya movement, Nawab Siddiq Hasan Khan wrote in his book, *Kashf al-Litham*, to this effect, admitting clearly that this condition of the 'ulama could be plainly witnessed at the present time. It is at least certain that the debasement of the 'ulama and the advent of the Messiah are described as contemporaneous events. Equally certain is it that the 'ulama in this age have done the greatest disservice to Islam by wrangling among themselves and wasting all national energy in internal dissensions and not caring in the least for the sufferings of Islam itself. They have entirely neglected their prime duty of upholding the cause of Islam as against the opposing forces and have brought further discredit

44. *Baihaqi.*
45. *Kanz al-'Ummal,* vol. vii, p. 190.

on it by their narrow-mindedness in fighting among
themselves on the most trivial points, [46] thus making
themselves and Islam itself, whose champions they
are supposed to be, the laughing-stock of the world.
If these people, when reminded of their duty,
turned against the man who was commissioned to
lead Islam to triumph and heaped all sorts of
abusive epithets upon him, thus hampering the great
work which he was to accomplish, he was justified
in calling them unworthy sons of Islam, and, in a
spiritual sense, the illegitimate offspring of their
great ancestors.

THE AHMADIYYA MOVEMENT

The Ahmadiyya movement as the West sees it

I will bring to a close this short study of the life
of the founder of the Ahmadiyya movement by
considering two more questions - Was he mad? Was
he insincere? I have read a book recently written
by an anonymous Shi'a writer which ends with the
considered view that Hazrat Mirza Ghulam Ahmad
was a madman. A madman could not build a house or

46. A very severe contest has been raging in the Muslim world over the
accent of the "Amen" recited after the Fatiha in prayers, the majority
holding that it should be pronounced in a low voice, and a small minority,
the Wahabis, holding that it should be pronounced loudly. How often has
the sacred and serene atmosphere of a congregational prayer been
disturbed by the taking-up of cudgels to belabour an unfortunate member
of the congregation who happened to pronounce the Amen aloud! Cases
have gone right up to High Courts of Judicature to determine the right of
one section to say their prayers in certain mosques which were built by
Muslims of another persuasion. Even this becomes insignificant when one
finds that a great struggle is carried on over the pronouncement of the
letter dzad, which some read as dad and others as zad, the real
pronunciation lying somewhere midway between the two, and fatwas of
kufr have been given against one another on a matter of which a man
possessing a grain of common sense would not take notice.

design a plan of the building of a house, and yet we are asked in all seriousness to accept it as a fact that the man who founded a movement and built up such an important community as the Ahmadiyya, was a madman. To call such a man mad is nothing but madness. I give a few brief quotations from recent Western writers showing what the Ahmadiyya movement is:

"They are a very remarkable group in modern Islam, the only group that has purely missionary aims. They are marked by a devotion, zeal and sacrifice that call for genuine admiration ... Their founder Mirza Ghulam Ahmad must have powerful personality." [47]

"Their mental energy is concentrated on painting Islam as upholder of broad, social and moral ideals." [48]

"Their vindication and defence of Islam is accepted by many educated Muslims as the form in which they can remain intellectually loyal to Islam." [49]

"The Ahmadis are at present the most active propagandists of Islam in the world." [50]

"The movement initiated by Mirza Ghulam Ahmad occupies a unique position in relation to both the orthodox party and the rationalistic reformers

47. *The Moslem World*, vol. xxi, p. 170.
48. *Ibid.*
49. *Op. cit.*, vol. xxi, p. 171.
50. *Indian Islam*, p. 217.

represented by Sir Syed Ahmad Khan and his Neo-Mutazilite followers. Ahmad himself declaimed bitterly against the professional Mullas of Islam who kept people in darkness, who had allowed Islam to die of formalism, who had not prevented the division into sects . . . At the same time he could not tolerate the rationalizing expositors of Islam such as Syed Amir Ali and Prof. S. Khuda Bakhsh, who were beginning to throw doubt on the Qur'an, as a perfect work of Divine revelation." [51]

"Here we find the newest and most aggressive forms of propaganda against Christianity which have ever originated, and from here a world-wide programme of Muslim Foreign Missions is being maintained and financed." [52]

"This religious movement through its own dynamic force has attracted wide attention and secured followers all over the world." [53]

"What is of more interest to the outside world than the beliefs of either branch and their relations with the orthodox is the vigorous life and the fervent missionizing character of the movement." [54]

"The doctrine of the Ahmadiyya is of a highly ethical character, and it directs itself particularly towards the intellectuals." [55]

51. *Indian Islam*, p. 222.
52. *Op.cit.*, p. 229.
53. *Whither Islam?*, p. 214.
54. *Op. cit.*, p. 217.

"How movements like the Ahmadiyya with its strong ethical powers and its no doubt deep religious feelings are able to exercise a certain influence beyond what are so far considered to be the frontiers of Muslim territory".[56]

"To it also belongs the credit for the development of a modern Moslem apologetic which . . . is far from negligible."[57]

"The movement resolved itself mainly into liberal Islam with the peculiarity that it has definitely propagandist spirit and feels confident that it can make an appeal to Western nations, an appeal which has already been made with some measure of success."[58]

Well-organized, intellectual movement

Can any sane person for a moment entertain the idea that a madman could bring to life such a strongly-organized, vigorous and rational movement?

The second question is - was he insincere? Here again I ask the reader to consider if an insincere man could produce such devoted and sincere followers? Insincerity could give birth only to insincerity, and it is the height of folly to call a man insincere who gathers about himself not only devoted and sincere but also intelligent men who are admittedly the best Muslim missionaries today,

55. *Whither Islam?*, p. 288.
56. *Op. cit.*, p. 309.
57. *Op. cit.*, p. 353.
58. *Islam at the Cross-roads*, p. 99.

and who are leading an admittedly intellectual movement. Moreover, the whole course of Hazrat Ahmad's life from early youth shows that he was devoted to the cause of the propagation of Islam. Again, an insincere man could not but have some ulterior motive, but the founder of the Ahmadiyya movement cannot be shown to have any such motive. After all, what did he gain by this so-called insincerity? He was at the height of his fame when he laid claim to Promised Messiahship, and he sacrificed by this claim the reputation which he had built for himself during half a century. An insincere man would have done his best to retain the fame which he had acquired and the honour in which he was held. Nor did he make any estate for himself. On the other hand, when he was informed that his end was nigh, he at once constituted a society to which he entrusted complete control of management and of finances. He did not care for the acquisition of either wealth or honour, and sincerity marks every step that he took for the building up of the cause of the propagation of Islam, even every word that he wrote. If such a man could be insincere, truly the world must have become devoid of sincere men!

THE AHMADIYYA MOVEMENT AS THE WEST SEES IT

Under this heading, near the close of the main body of this book, Maulana Muhammad Ali has collected extracts from the writings of Western scholars regarding the Ahmadiyya Movement and its Holy Founder. This Appendix gives some further extracts on the subject from more recent Western opinion.

In the New Edition of the *Encyclopaedia of Islam*[1], compiled by a board of eminent Western orientalists, Professor Wilfred Cantwell Smith says of the Ahmadiyya Anjuman Isha'at Islam, Lahore:

"It has been active in a systematic and effective fashion, chiefly in three overlapping fields: publishing, organized foreign missionary work, and leadership in intellectual modernism (liberalism) in Islam, especially of English-reading Islam. It has produced and circulated throughout the world (chiefly in English and Urdu, but also in a half-dozen and more other European and well over a dozen Asian languages) translations of the Quran, lives of Muhammad, impressive expositions of Islam, many monographs and essays, and innumerable pamphlets. Its foreign missions, in London, Berlin, Indonesia, have been influential . . ." (Under entry *Ahmadiyya*, p. 302, column 2.)

In the voluminous scholarly work *Religion in the*

Middle East[2], the author of the chapter *The Ahmadis*[3], James Robson, Emeritus Professor of Arabic at the University of Manchester, includes the following observations about Hazrat Mirza Ghulam Ahmad:

"[in his youth] he spent most of his time studying his own and other religions, showing great distaste for the legal disputes about property which his father urged him to undertake. He was an ardent Muslim who longed for the regeneration of Islam ... " (p. 349)

"Muslims commonly believe that a reformer is sent at the beginning of each century, and Ghulam Ahmad appeared to some to be the reformer (*mujaadid*) of the fourteenth century. He began to write a voluminous work, *Barahin Ahmadiyya* (Ahmadi proofs), the early parts of which were welcomed by Muslims who read them ... " (p. 351)

"... to many he was an attractive personality, a persuasive speaker and writer with an appealing message. He held that he had been sent to recall mankind to orthodox Islam ... He held that the Quran was unique, much superior to the Bible ... He insisted that revelation has not ceased with Muhammad, but was careful to explain that his inspiration was not like that of the Quran." (p. 352)

Regarding the Ahmadiyya Anjuman Isha'at Islam, Lahore, the chapter continues:

"This party has conducted a vigorous missionary and literary programme. (Khwaja) Kamal-ud-Din came to England and was *imam* of the Woking mosque, editor of the *Islamic Review* and author of many books in which he waged a vigorous propaganda against Christianity . . .

"The ideals of the party are stated to be the service of Islam, the unity, defence and propagation of Islam . . . Its beliefs are the finality of prophethood in Muhammad, the Quran as God's final and perfect book . . . that all who profess belief in God and His Messenger, whatever their school of thought in Islam, are Muslims, that Ghulam Ahmad is the *mujaddid* of the fourteenth century, and that he stated he laid no claim to prophethood" (p. 362).

Freeland Abbott, in his study of the modern history of Islam in Pakistan and in pre-partition India, entitled *Islam and Pakistan*[4], makes the following comments:

"In the third part [of *Barahin Ahmadiyya*], published in 1882, Ghulam Ahmad claimed to have received a revelation from God that he was the great reformer of Islam's fourteenth century – the *mujaddid* of his time . . . Even this does not seem to have disturbed the traditionalist theologians – an indication, perhaps, of the respect with which they accepted his book" (p. 150).

"Ghulam Ahmad's efforts were not only

defensive; he took the offensive as well, and established an extensive, highly organised missionary enterprise to carry the truths of Islam as he understood them to all parts of the world" (p. 152).

"The primary significance of the Ahmadiyya movement lay in its missionary emphasis ... The Ahmadiyyas made it part of their principles ... to proselytize energetically for Islam ...
    "In the course of time the Ahmadiyya arguments against other religions were wholeheartedly accepted by even their most vociferous [Muslim] critics ... Through the vigour of their proselytizing and their incessant and highly publicized attacks on Christianity, they instilled a stronger faith in many Muslims. They developed a confident belief that Christianity does not explain the strength of Europe, and that the true religion remained Islam ... This is the essential significance of the Ahmadiyya Movement. It is somewhat ironic that the sect most attacked by Muslims in India and Pakistan has also been that which has worked hardest, in both its branches, to defend and extend Islam against the competition offered by other faiths" (pp. 160, 161).

1. Luzac & Co., London, 1960.
2. General Editor, Professor. A. J. Arberry, published by the Cambridge University Press, 1968.
3. Ch. 19 in vol. 2, pp. 349-362.
4. Cornell University Press, U.S.A., 1968.